WINNERS

JUMPERS TO FOLLOW – 2023–24

Sixty-second year of publication

Contributors:
Rodney Pettinga
Richard Young

RACING POST

Commissioned by RACING POST, Floor 7, Vivo Building South Bank Central, 30 Stamford Street, London, SE1 9LS

First published in 2023 by PITCH PUBLISHING Ltd
9 Donnington Park, 85 Birdham Road, Chichester, West Sussex, PO20 7AJ
Order line: 01933 304 858

ISBN 978-1839501432

Printed and bound in Great Britain by Buxton Press Limited.

100 WINNERS
JUMPERS TO FOLLOW 2023-24
(ages as at 2023)

AFADIL (FR) 4 b g
French Flat winner Afadil looks just the sort to win
a good handicap over hurdles in the coming season.
Following two comfortable wins on his first two starts
for Paul Nicholls at Taunton (soft) in January and
at Musselburgh (good) a month later, he progressed
steadily in handicaps, starting with a creditable
eighth behind Jazzy Matty in the Boodles Juvenile
Handicap Hurdle (formerly known as the Fred
Winter) and culminating in a return to winning ways
at Ayr's Scottish National meeting. The Swinton was
mooted as a possible option following that race but he
sidestepped the race and connections can look forward
to a profitable 2023-24 season with a horse who has
a stack of physical scope. He's yet to race over further
than 2m but there's a good chance he'll improve for
longer trips and, given his age and the fact that he
starts the season on a workable mark of 128, it'll be
no surprise to see a decent prize or two head his way.
PAUL NICHOLLS

AN EPIC SONG (FR) 6 b g

When An Epic Song won over 2m3f at Punchestown in December 2021 – in the process landing a bit of a gamble – he looked just the sort who could step up to the mark at one of the handicaps at the big spring festivals in 2022. However, he wasn't seen out again until December of that year, when he started at a big price and looked in need of the run in a Fairyhouse handicap back at 2m. It was a similar story over the same trip at the Dublin Festival in February but he stepped up appreciably on both those efforts when a fine second in first-time tongue-tie/cheekpieces in the ultra-competitive Coral Cup at Cheltenham, only a head behind Langer Dan. On the back of that run he started 11/2 second favourite for a similar handicap at Punchestown but he was nearest at the finish in ninth over the shorter trip having been hampered by a faller early doors. He should stay 3m and, whether he keeps to hurdles or goes chasing this season, he looks one to follow. MARTIN BRASSIL

APPLE AWAY (IRE) 6 b m

Ahoy Senor won the Grade 1 Sefton Novices' Hurdle for Lucinda Russell in 2021, a race where he announced his arrival on the big stage by turning over Bravemansgame on what was just his second start over hurdles. Russell repeated the trick in 2023 with Apple Away, another winning Irish pointer, and this mare is another fine prospect for Grade 1 chasing honours this term. She ran seven times in 2022-23, winning four, but she improved for stepping up to around 3m in the second half of the season, winning her last three starts, including that Aintree Grade 1 in April. Russell said afterwards: "I'm so delighted with Apple Away. She's relentless, she just keeps on galloping. Stephen (Mulqueen) did a very good job in kicking early and getting that lead. I wasn't worried at the last this time, she's a total three-miler. When we came into the race we knew that she had a few pounds to find but the mares' allowance is ideal and she's just got such tenacity and determination which is ideal for this sort of race." That tenacity and determination will also stand her in good stead as she embarks on her chasing career and she's one to keep onside. LUCINDA RUSSELL

ASCENDING (IRE) 4 b g

Although Ascending only won once on the Flat for Clive Cox (over 1m at Goodwood on soft), he was a consistent sort who achieved a peak BHA rating of 82. He also showed plenty of ability in his new career over hurdles for his new team and, although he didn't win in three hurdle starts, he showed more than enough to suggest he can rectify matters in the coming months. Having cost his new owners 100,000gns, he jumped adequately on his hurdling debut at Leopardstown in December, pushing Tekao, the Willie Mullins-trained market leader, all the way to the line, the pair almost four lengths clear of the remainder. After that encouraging display he was stepped up markedly in class but he shaped with promise in Grade 1 events at the Dublin Festival in February and when finishing fifth to Lossiemouth in the Triumph Hurdle at Cheltenham the following month. Whether he tries to win a maiden / novice or goes straight into handicaps remains to be seen, but he's open to a fair bit of improvement given his tender age and his opening handicap mark of 133 looks one that his excellent trainer should be able to exploit. HENRY DE BROMHEAD

AURORA VEGA (IRE) 5 b m

A daughter of Quevega and a sister to quadruple Grade 1-winner Facile Vega (who is also by Walk In The Park), Aurora Vega made her racecourse debut in an ordinary 2m2f Sligo bumper in June where she easily justified odds of 1/5 by running out a comfortable 12-length winner, having taken it up 2f out. Her rider Patrick Mullins said afterwards: "Aurora Vega is like her mother, quite small and short but she's a strong barrel of a mare. She's not the flashiest at home but I think she's probably better than her work and I think there's more there in the tank, she's one that will keep giving." She won again in late August, beating a field of inferior rivals as she liked at Killarney at odds of 1/7 and, as at Sligo, she never had to come out of a canter. It's early days with her of course, but she could prove to be an ideal type for the Mares' Novices' Hurdle on the Thursday of the Cheltenham Festival, for which she is currently available at 14/1. That race has only existed since 2016 and Willie Mullins has already won it five times so he certainly knows what it takes. WILLIE MULLINS

AUTUMN RETURN (IRE) 6 b m

A 3m Irish point winner in early 2022 and a bumper winner on her first start for Ruth Jefferson (after changing hands for £55,000) in April of that year, Autumn Return got her hurdling career off to a perfect start that autumn by winning a mares' novices' hurdle over 2m 125y at Market Rasen. Among the beaten horses were Mullenburg and Kingston Sunflower, both of whom would go and win three races on the spin subsequently. She ran creditably under a penalty at Wetherby a month later, finishing fourth of eleven behind Hall Lane and that race has worked out fairly well with six of the beaten horses all winning at least one race afterwards. Autumn Return was outclassed behind Luccia in a Listed race at Newbury in November but 2m on good ground was probably not her thing and she bounced back to winning form on soft ground at Catterick at the end of December, beating Bents Hollow, who is a decent yardstick, by 4l despite carrying a 7lb penalty. She finished second on her handicap debut at Newcastle one month later, where she probably matched her Catterick performance but she already looked in need of a stiffer test when finishing fourth behind Bonttay in a decent handicap hurdle over

2m at Kelso on soft ground in late March. Upped to 2m4f at Perth on her final start of the season a month later, she won another mares' handicap in good style. She is rated 115 after that and she looks capable of adding to her tally over 2m4f+ in the early part of the season but, given her pointing background, she also has the option of chasing and she looks sure to win races in that discipline. RUTH JEFFERSON

BALLYBURN (IRE) 5 b g

Given the stamina in Ballyburn's pedigree it's highly encouraging that he was able to win both his starts in bumpers over 2m earlier this year. This 3m point winner, who started second favourite, created a fine impression (despite pulling hard) when successful on his rules debut at Punchestown in February, beating fancied runners from the Gordon Elliott and Eddie O'Grady yards. He stepped up on that form back at the same venue during their Festival week in April, racing with the choke out again but powering clear in the closing stages to beat two previous winners, Dancing City and Slade Steel, by upwards of six lengths. He'll likely need further to show his very best once he goes over hurdles and as such, at this stage looks much more a Ballymore type (7/1 favourite at the time of writing) than he does a Supreme Novice one. His wins were achieved on yielding and good to yielding and, although his longer term future obviously lies over fences, he is a really exciting prospect for the season ahead. WILLIE MULLINS

BERTIE B 5 b g

Clive Boultbee-Brooks is a Herefordshire-based point-to-point trainer but he also has a decent strike-rate under rules and in Bertie B he has an inmate who should pay his way over hurdles this term. Out of a half-sister to Agnese, a bumper winner who was the dam of Lieutenant Colonel, a Grade 1-winning hurdler in Ireland, Bertie

B won a Bangor bumper in April 2022, but he didn't cut much ice in his first two hurdles starts in late 2022 and early 2023. However, he very much caught the eye at 66/1 in a 2m6f event at Hereford in late January, where he finished fifth of twelve behind Atlanta Brave without being given too hard a time by his rider. He then ran in a handicap the following month over 2m4f at Huntingdon and he again acquitted himself with credit, finishing a close third of eleven behind Blue Shark, who was completing a five-timer. There were two subsequent winners in behind so the form looks strong. Bertie B was raised 3lb by the handicapper despite only finishing third but his new mark of 105 looks workable and he should get going in this discipline sooner rather than later.

CLIVE BOULTBEE-BROOKS

BLAZING KHAL (IRE) 7 b g

This gelding won his first three races over hurdles in late 2021, including two Grade 2 contests at Cheltenham over 2m5f and 3m and, following the second of those two wins in December 2021, he was installed as the warm ante-post favourite for the Albert Bartlett Novices' Hurdle at the Cheltenham Festival, which Charles Byrnes also won with future RSA Chase winner Weapons Amnesty in 2009. However, a setback forced Blazing Khal to miss that engagement and ultimately he was forced off the track for fourteen months, with Byrnes admitting that it took longer to get him right than had been expected. His eagerly-awaited comeback came in the Grade 2 Boyne Hurdle at Navan in mid-February and he didn't disappoint, running out a 3l winner from Meet And Greet with the likes of Beacon Edge, Sire Du Berlais and Saint Sam further behind. With improvement expected after such a long absence, he was immediately installed as one of the favourites for the Stayers' Hurdle at Cheltenham a month later. However, he suffered a cut to a fetlock while winning the Boyne and his preparation was therefore interrupted again, with Byrnes only declaring him fit to run at Prestbury Park about a week before the Stayers' Hurdle. He acquitted himself well in the race, finishing sixth behind Sire Du Berlais after getting tired in the closing stages but one feels that it might have been a different story had his preparation gone more smoothly. Before his comeback, Byrnes had been toying with a switch to fences for the 7yo and perhaps now is the time to make that change, as he still has time on his side. He's a 33/1 shot for the Cheltenham Gold Cup, which is perhaps a bit fanciful, but the 20/1 on offer for the Brown Advisory Novices Chase (formerly known as the RSA chase) looks like a fair price, provided that he stays fit and healthy. CHARLES BYRNES

BOWENSPARK (IRE) 5 b g

Henry Daly, just like his old guv'nor Captain Tim Forster, tends to excel with late-developing staying types and he has one that falls firmly into that category in Bowenspark, who deserves plenty of credit for being able to win twice and gain Graded-placed status in bumpers in his first season. The 5yo, who carries the colours of the late Trevor Hemmings, did well to win on his first two starts at Uttoxeter and Warwick (both races threw up subsequent winners) at the end of 2022 and, although he was unable to add to his tally, he shaped promisingly in Listed company at Newbury in February and in a good-quality Grade 2 at Aintree on his final start, despite the muddling gallop for much of the journey being against him. He will be suited by at least 2m4f once he goes over obstacles and, although chasing will eventually be his game, it'll be a surprise if he doesn't acquit himself with credit in some of the better hurdle races this time round. HENRY DALY

BRANDY MCQUEEN (IRE) 6 b g

Harriet Graham wouldn't exactly be a household name for those who are based more towards the south of the country but this clerk-of-the-course cum racehorse trainer has proved herself a capable operator in both spheres. Smart staying chaser Aye Right has blown the trumpet for both herself and co-trainer Gary Rutherford in recent times and, although Brandy McQueen has a long way to go before he gets to that level, he'll be interesting if sent over fences in the current campaign. The 6yo held his form well in a busy season in 2022-23, winning back-to-back races in May 2022 and repeating that feat at Musselburgh in the early part of this year, before finishing a highly respectable seventh to Good Time Jonny in the Pertemps Final at the Cheltenham Festival. He'd probably had enough for the season when disappointing at Ayr on his final start but he's bred to jump a fence, he seems to handle most ground and he'll be of interest in staying handicap chases. HARRIET GRAHAM & GARY RUTHERFORD

BRIGHTERDAYSAHEAD (FR) 4 b f

An aptly-named half-sister to the yard's ill-fated triple Grade 1 winner Mighty Potter, Brighterdaysahead won a 2m1f Gowran Park bumper in February by 13l and, while it wasn't the strongest race with her two main market rivals failing to produce their true running, she could do no more than win in the manner she did. Her next outing would tell us more and she didn't disappoint as she ran out a 4l winner of an 18-runner Fairyhouse contest over 2m in early April, with a couple of the beaten horses running well subsequently to uphold the form. That victory came just half an hour after Mighty Potter lost his life when taking a heavy fall in the Grade 1 chase on the same card and Gordon Elliott obviously had mixed emotions afterwards: "Everyone is very upset after Mighty Potter but on a brighter note this is a seriously good mare. It's bittersweet, but Brighterdaysahead is a mare we can look forward to over the summer. That'll be her for the season now and you won't see her again until

next spring." She's one to look out for in novice hurdles and she looks nailed on to win more races.
GORDON ELLIOTT

BYKER (IRE) 4 b g

Byker was picked up for 25,000gns by shrewd Irish trainer Charles Byrnes following his good-ground Windsor victory for Richard Hannon in October 2022. It immediately looked like money well spent when he ran out a cosy winner of a Naas maiden hurdle on only his second start for his new trainer the following February. Although beaten when returning to the same track under a penalty next time, he turned in his best effort in first-time cheekpieces when a neck second to Jazzy Matty in the Boodles Juvenile Handicap Hurdle (formerly the Fred Winter) on his handicap debut at the Cheltenham Festival, keeping on strongly in the closing stages to finish ahead of two subsequent scorers in a race that also threw up a couple of other winners. His only run since came in the valuable Swinton Handicap Hurdle at Haydock in May and he ran well again to finish fifth in a competitive renewal against older handicappers. He shapes as though he'll stay a bit further and he has plenty of handicapping scope from his current rating.
CHARLES BYRNES

CAPTAIN TEAGUE (IRE) 5 ch g

Captain Teague only ran twice in bumpers last term but he ended up as one of the best performers in that sphere courtesy of a fine third to A Dream To Share, the division's best performer of the season, at the Cheltenham Festival in March. In a race dominated by the Irish, the Paul Nicholls-trained 5yo caused interference to a few of his rivals by hanging left in the closing stages (earning Harry Cobden a four-day ban) but he still stuck on pluckily to get within two and a half lengths of John Kiely's unbeaten runner, earning himself a 33/1 quote for this season's Supreme Novices Hurdle and a 25/1 one for the Ballymore. Although this point winner has stamina in his pedigree and should stay at least 2m4f, he's also not short of speed (he's a half-brother to smart 2m chaser Sky Pirate), so it'll be interesting to see which route his trainer chooses for him. Whichever path is trod, it will be surprising if it doesn't turn out to be a fruitful one. PAUL NICHOLLS

CHASING FIRE 6 b g

Chasing Fire was found out when he went up in grade over hurdles last season but he still showed enough to suggest that he remains one to keep an eye on in the coming months. This point and bumper winner won his first three starts over hurdles – justifying odds-on favouritism on each start – at Market Rasen (twice) and at Sandown before coming up short in the Supreme Novices' Hurdle, where he finished twelfth of fourteen. He appreciated the switch back to the non-graded novice company on his final start at Cheltenham's April meeting where he ran well to finish third to The Friday Man over 2m4f, one place behind subsequent hurdle and chase winner Twig. Before the Supreme his trainer intimated that this highly-regarded sort will be a very good chaser for this season so presumably he'll be starting off in the new discipline. He handles good and soft ground, is open to improvement and should be able to make his mark in novice company over fences. OLLY MURPHY

CHASING UNICORN (IRE) 5 b g

The green silks of Simon Munir and Isaac Souede have become a familiar sight on British and Irish racecourses both over jumps and, more frequently of late, on the Flat. They'll likely have a strong hand in several departments for this jumps season and it'll be a surprise should the once-raced bumper winner Chasing Unicorn not contribute to their tally of wins at some stage. Despite a starting price of 25/1, the 5yo was professional on his debut in a Punchestown bumper in April, where he stayed on too strongly in the closing stages for the Charles Byrnes-trained newcomer Intent Approach. Although the bare form of that 2m event is nothing out of the ordinary, Chasing Unicorn is by Mahler out of a Presenting mare so it's reasonable to assume there'll be a good deal of improvement when he goes over hurdles over 2m4f and beyond. He looks a useful prospect. S R B CRAWFORD

CHOSEN WITNESS (IRE) 6 b g

Although Chosen Witness was a well-beaten 66/1 shot in the Champion Bumper at Cheltenham in March, he showed more than enough in his other starts in bumpers last season to suggest he'll be winning races when he gets a trip over hurdles this season. This debut point winner was a shade off odds-on for his debut in his new discipline at Limerick in late December 2022 and bolted up in an admittedly ordinary contest, making all and coming clear of his rivals in the closing stages. He had his limitations exposed in Graded company on his next run at the Dublin Festival, though he was far from disgraced in that Grade 2 event behind A Dream To Share, who would go on to win Grade 1s at Cheltenham and at Punchestown. It's safe to put a line through his Cheltenham run and he's instead better judged on his Punchestown run in a non-graded event on his final start, where he finished in a dead-heat for fourth behind three previous winners. His pedigree suggests that he should stay well – his dam is from the family of Cheltenham Gold Cup winner Captain Christy – and he should be seen to good effect over 2m4f and beyond in the coming months. WILLIE MULLINS

CITY CHIEF (IRE) 6 b g

The Coral Gold Cup (formerly the Hennessy) at Newbury in early December looks the perfect early-season target for City Chief, who quickly made up into a smart staying chaser last season. There's the promise of much more to come too, especially as there's still room for improvement in the jumping department, as he showed when making a few errors at Ayr on his final start when third to wide-margin winner Sail Away on ground (good) that would have been plenty quick enough for him. Prior to that he'd created a favourable impression by winning at Hereford in January and at Wetherby in February. On the latter occasion he jumped soundly and made all, finishing some five lengths ahead of previous Newcastle scorer O'Toole. James Bowen, who rode him in that Grade 2 contest, said he still had some growing up to do and he'll likely be a stronger and more streetwise performer this time round. He's only six, he's had just ten starts under rules and he's in excellent hands, so it's a fair bet that there's more improvement to come. NICKY HENDERSON

COOPER'S CROSS (IRE) 8 b g

The 2022-23 season was the best one from a prize-money point of view for Scottish Borders trainer Stuart Coltherd – his eighteen winners amassed prize money of just over £300,000, a good chunk of that total provided courtesy of Cooper's Cross. The gelding won twice last season, including the valuable Sky Bet Chase at Doncaster in first-time cheekpieces in January, before finishing an excellent second to Eider and subsequent Bet365 Gold Cup winner Kitty's Light in the Scottish National on his final start in April. The handicapper had little choice but to raise him a further 3lb for that Ayr run but he'll remain of interest in all the big staying events in 2023-24, though his record suggests he'd unlikely want the ground to become too deep. He fell four out in the Topham at Aintree in April, but he'd jumped the National fences well up to that point and it wouldn't be a surprise should he be given another go over them at some stage this season.
STUART COLTHERD

CORBETTS CROSS (IRE) 6 ch g

Stay Away Fay was an impressive all-the-way winner of the Grade 1 Albert Bartlett Novices' Hurdle over 3m for Paul Nicholls at Cheltenham in March but it may well have been a different story if Corbetts Cross hadn't jinked right before running out at the last flight of hurdles. At the time he was about 1l down on the leader but he'd not yet been asked for maximum effort so it's anyone's guess whether he would have got up the hill better than his rival, but in either case it was still a tremendous run in a Grade 1. Prior to that, the chestnut had already won a Grade 2 over just shy of 2m at Naas in February, which was his first run for Emmet Mullins, having been switched to him after a brace of hurdles wins for his previous trainer Eugene O'Sullivan, one a maiden hurdle over 2m5f at Limerick in December and the other a handicap hurdle over 3m at Fairyhouse in January. Now owned by JP McManus, this 3m point winner at Kildorrery in February 2022 has always been thought of as more of a chasing prospect so it's to his great credit that he has come so far over a variety of trips and on a variety of ground over hurdles. Before Cheltenham he'd displayed no wayward tendencies but his trainer did describe him as a "quirky individual" in a pre-race interview, which is something to bear in mind. The trainer said afterwards: "He came out of it okay, we'll get him home and let him relax and try to get him going early next season. I don't know what happened, I haven't watched the replay back. We'll just put it down as one of those things and move on to next year. He'll be going over fences this term and coming from the point-to-point field he's a great prospect." There should be plenty of good days for him in the future and he's firmly one to follow.

EMMET MULLINS

DESERT HEATHER (IRE) 7 b m

The winner of three points not long after joining Declan Queally in late 2022, Desert Heather also ran some great races over hurdles between late December and mid-May, winning two and placing in three others. Second over 2m3f on her hurdle debut at Limerick at the end of 2022, she fell a month later over a similar trip at Fairyhouse when looking booked for another placed finish. She then ran well to finish third behind two next-time-out winners over 2m6f at Punchestown in February before another close second behind Fortunefavorsbold over 3m at Limerick in March. A rare poor run followed at Clonmel in early April but she may not have been suited by a drop back to 2m3f 106y on that occasion. She was given an official rating of 106 after that run and she made light of it on her handicap debut over 2m7f at Kilbeggan two weeks later, winning as she liked from a field of seasoned handicappers. She followed up three weeks later at the same course over slightly further off a 14lb higher mark, edging out Desertmore House, who would go on to win a beginners' chase by 10l on his next outing, with a further 9l back to the third. She may be kept to handicap hurdles to start with this season but, given her pointing background, a return to fences will surely happen at some stage with her trainer describing her as "hard as nails" which will stand her in good stead as she re-embarks on that part of her career. DECLAN QUEALLY

DOUGLAS TALKING (IRE) 7 b g

Who says the north can't compete with the south in the jumping sphere anymore? Not Lucinda Russell, who was on the mark at the most recent Cheltenham and Aintree Festivals with Corach Rambler (Ultima/Grand National winner) and Grade 1 scorer Apple Away. Douglas Talking also stepped up a fair way on the form he'd shown in the previous season, winning 2m handicap chases at Ayr and Sandown in February and March respectively before finishing second at Aintree and Punchestown in April. A wind operation in late 2022 was the key to his progress this year and he wouldn't have to improve too much to make his mark in Listed or minor Graded company, especially in small fields where he's able to dominate. He's an experienced chaser with a good strike-rate for one of his age (five wins from ten runs) and he looks set for a good season, especially if he can iron out the jumping errors shown on his last two starts (both in double-figure fields). LUCINDA RUSSELL

DOWN MEMORY LANE (IRE) 5 b g

The winner of a 3m maiden point at Umma House for Jonathan and Mikey Fogarty in October 2022, this Walk In The Park gelding was reunited with Derek O'Connor on his first run for Gordon Elliott four months later as he took part in a Fairyhouse bumper over 2m and half a furlong. Travelling strongly in midfield, he made stylish progress as they reached the home turn and he then ran on willingly when asked to win his race in the closing stages, ultimately prevailing by an easy four-and-a-half lengths. The form worked out splendidly with the second and third both winning a bumper next time and three of the horses who finished further behind also won over hurdles subsequently. Clearly the experience of his point win had benefited him greatly with O'Connor describing him as "very professional and nice and relaxed." He's now racing in the colours of JP McManus and he could take a high rank as a hurdler – it would be no surprise to see him at this season's Cheltenham Festival, with the Albert Bartlett Novices' Hurdle perhaps the logical target, given that he stayed 3m well in his point. GORDON ELLIOTT

DYSART ENOS (IRE) 5 b m

Bought for £95,000 at the Goffs UK sales in April 2022 after finishing second in an Irish point a month earlier, Dysart Enos made a promising start to her career in late November at Ludlow when running out the convincing winner of a 15-runner bumper. She next took on the highly-touted Queens Gamble, who had created such a favourable impression at Cheltenham when winning a Listed mares' bumper, in another Listed contest over an extended 2m at Market Rasen in February. She won going away by a length from that good benchmark and there were two other future winners among the beaten horses, so the form has a rock-solid look to it. Dysart Enos next went to Aintree for the Grade 2 Mares' bumper over 2m1f and she posted an even more impressive display, beating her nineteen rivals in clear-cut fashion having cruised all the way round. The third horse, Williamstowndancer, has already won twice over hurdles and the race looks sure to throw up its usual share of winners. Fergal O'Brien was delighted with his mare: "We were hopeful coming here after Dysart Enos was very impressive at Market Rasen, but she was phenomenal today and that was beyond what we hoped. She's cruised all the way through. She's a good jumper too." She ran over 3m in her Irish point so there is plenty to look forward to with her over hurdles, especially when she starts stepping up in trip. FERGAL O'BRIEN

FACILE VEGA (IRE) 6 b g

After Facile Vega won the Champion Bumper at the Cheltenham Festival in March 2022, Willie Mullins said the following: "I've compared him to Florida Pearl, who was a very good bumper horse, and that's how highly we regard him. He'd be in the top percentage of our winners of this race." He started off well over hurdles too, winning an 18-runner maiden hurdle at Fairyhouse in early December and adding a Grade 1 at Leopardstown at the end of the month, in which he beat stablemates Il Etait Temps and Ashroe Diamond, who both won Graded races next time out. However, he then bombed out as the 4/9 favourite in the Grade 1 Tattersall Ireland Novice Hurdle at the Dublin Racing Festival in February, where he went off at a rate of knots with High Definition and he had nothing more to give before the final flight, eventually being eased to finish more than 20l behind runaway winner Il Etait Temps. The trainer felt that it was simply a case of going off too fast and Facile Vega also returned sore but he was still on a bit of a recovery mission as he lined up for the Supreme Novices' Hurdle six weeks later. This time he settled far better and looked all set to win as he took it up two out but he may have gone too early and he was ultimately no match for Marine Nationale after he stumbled at the last. Six weeks afterwards he won his second Grade 1 (his fourth when you include bumpers) at Punchestown, getting the better of his old adversary Il Etait Temps, although that rival made a bad mistake early which may well have affected the outcome. Facile Vega also made an error three out but he recovered to win going away and Willie Mullins said afterwards: "Paul (Townend) thinks Facile Vega doesn't have any respect for hurdles, so the sooner we go chasing the better. Paul said all season he's been capable of doing something like that. He did it at Cheltenham and did it today, and we'll pop him over a fence maybe next week and put him out to grass and then come back over fences next season. He's got a huge engine and huge stride. His back pedigree is all stamina and staying, and it's fantastic he's able to win Grade 1 races over two miles, but I'd have no problem if he tells us he can go over two and a half or even three miles over fences." Look out for him in all the top novice events this season and, given those trainer comments, quotes of 7/1 for the Brown Advisory Novices' Chase over 2m4f look far more tempting than the 6/1 which is currently his best price for the Arkle. WILLIE MULLINS

FACT TO FILE (FR) 6 b g

The winner of a Bellharbour point in February 2022, Fact To File was well backed to make a winning debut under rules when lining up for a Leopardstown bumper over 2m4f in December. Irish Panther appeared to have his measure for most of the last half mile in that contest before Fact To File's stamina reserves kicked in and he got on top late to win going away by 2l. He next went off as favourite for the Grade 2 bumper at the Dublin Racing Festival in early February but he had to give best to A Dream To Share in that 2m contest and it was the same story in the Champion Bumper at the Cheltenham Festival six weeks later, although he did get a little bit closer to his rival on the second occasion. In both of those contests he was keeping on well in the closing stages having been outpaced, giving notice that he's likely to excel over longer trips as a hurdler. Given that A Dream To Share is a remarkable bumper horse who won five on the spin in just under a year, Fact To File really did very little wrong in finishing second to him twice and he rates a high-class prospect as a hurdler this season. The Albert Bartlett over 3m on the Friday of Cheltenham looks a suitable long-term target for him and you could argue that 10/1 is a fair price, even at this early juncture. Looking further ahead, he could develop into a genuine Gold Cup horse in a couple of seasons. WILLIE MULLINS

FARLAND (IRE) 4 b g

A half-brother to Minella Cocooner, a Grade 1 winner over hurdles, Farland is out of a dam who also won at Graded level over both hurdles and fences. He was well backed to make a winning debut for Sean Doyle in the Goffs Defender Bumper at the Punchestown Festival in late April, but he made things very difficult for his pilot Derek O'Connor by running green before leaning to the left inside the final furlong, ultimately ending up on the near rail. The race had gotten away from him by this stage but he still kept on well to finish fourth of the sixteen runners behind Predators Gold. The experience will have done him the world of good and he remains a fine prospect for hurdling this season as there is clearly a decent engine in him. He's bred to stay well. SEAN THOMAS DOYLE

FAVOUR AND FORTUNE (IRE) 5 br g

Given the stamina in Favour And Fortune's pedigree it's highly encouraging that he was able to win his first two starts in 2m bumpers last season. He was well found in the market on his racecourse debut at Southwell (soft) in November and took advantage of the below-par showing of the short-priced favourite when beating Spago by just over five lengths, with a bigger gap back to the rest of the field. He stepped up on that effort in a race comprising four previous winners at Warwick on good ground nearly three months later, travelling strongly before pulling over seven lengths clear of Alright Dai. He was found out when upped markedly in grade on his final start in the Champion Bumper at Cheltenham but he was far from disgraced and he looks the type to make up into a useful hurdler in the coming season, with trips of 2m4f and beyond likely to see him in a more favourable light. His trainer is unlikely to be rushing him but he's one to look forward to. ALAN KING

FERONILY (IRE) 6 b g

Sold for £45,000 at the Tatts November sale in Cheltenham shortly after winning a 3m maiden point at Rathcannon in November 2022, Feronily has since come a long way in a short time for owner Paul Byrne and trainer Emmet Mullins. He finished second behind an odds-on shot trained by Willie Mullins in a 2m Leopardstown bumper in late December, with subsequent wide-margin Down Royal winner No Time To Wait back in third. He then ran in the Grade 2 bumper at the Dublin Racing Festival in February where he finished third behind A Dream To Share and Fact To File and those two horses would royally frank that form next time out by again finishing 1-2 in the Grade 1 bumper at Cheltenham a month later. Feronily was again pitched into the deep end for his hurdling debut in early March and he acquitted himself well as he finished fourth

behind Nemean Lion in the Grade 2 Premier Novices'
Hurdle over 2m2f at Kelso, a bad blunder two out not
helping his cause as he was still in with every chance at
the time. He built on that by winning a maiden hurdle
at Limerick (2m3f) at the end of the same month but
his trainer was already looking at a chasing career for
his charge: "Feronily has a lot of potential and he will
probably go over fences next season. He is six years of
age and there was no point waiting until next year to stay
novice hurdling." We actually saw him over fences just
two weeks later in a Grade 3 contest at Cork where he
finished second behind Bachasson, beaten by just three-
and-a-quarter lengths, with none other than six-time
Grade 1 winner Chacun Pour Soi just behind him. That
was some race for one having his first chase start under
rules and he quickly built on it by beating Appreciate
It, James Du Berlais, Classic Getaway, Sir Gerhard and
Journey With Me in the Grade 1 Champion Novice
Chase at Punchestown at the end of April. Mullins said
afterwards: "Feronily is progressing with each run and is
an exciting horse to have. He's such a good jumper and we
saw that in the point-to-point field, which was part of the
reason why we purchased him. We weren't going to waste
time (over hurdles) as we knew we had a horse who was
progressing and we wanted to get the most out of him."
He ran another good race back over hurdles at Auteuil in
late May but surely the focus of the new season will be
chasing and there are clearly some decent prizes to be
won with him – don't rule out a Gold Cup tilt in March if
he continues his progression. EMMET MULLINS

FILEY BAY (IRE) 7 b g

In a relatively short space of time Emmet Mullins has
shown himself to be a high-class addition to the training
ranks. He was bred for the job being the nephew of
multiple Champion Irish trainer Willie Mullins and,
in 2022, he achieved what most trainers fail to do in a

lifetime when he won the Grand National with Noble Yeats. Although Filey Bay is operating further down the food chain than that illustrious stable companion, he looks just the type to win a decent handicap over hurdles this season. He won his first two starts for the yard (following a 400+ day absence) last November and December before finishing a fine second in the Grade 3 Betfair Hurdle at Newbury in February. That effort was matched when he finished third in the County Hurdle at Cheltenham the following month and, after a spin on the Flat, he shaped as though he retained all of his ability with a solid fifth in the competitive Galway Hurdle. He faced a straightforward task when winning on the Flat at Tramore later in August and, although beaten in a first-time hood dropped to an extended 7f at Tipperary in early September (the run can easily be forgiven), that should have teed him up nicely for a shot at some of the season's bigger jump handicaps in Britain and Ireland. Given his pedigree, it wouldn't be a surprise if we saw him jump a fence at some point. EMMET MULLINS

FLEMENSFACE (IRE) 6 b g

The easy winner of a 3m point at Knockanohill in March, Flemensface then ran in a 2m3f bumper at Cork a month later and he put up a smart performance as he won going away. The third and fourth both won next time out to boost the form and his trainer at the time, Michael Griffin said: "Flemensface is as good as I've trained and a brilliant jumper of a fence. He is for sale." Shortly afterwards, he was snapped up at the Cheltenham sales by Lucinda Russell and Paul McIvor for £100,000 and he will now go novice hurdling for his new owners, Richard and Katherine Gilbert. His brother Flemenstide won a bumper and a novice hurdle for Paul Nicholls, and there's every chance that this gelding could prove at least as good as that horse. His return to action is eagerly awaited and he appeals as the type to run up a sequence in non-handicap hurdles in the north before going on to better things. LUCINDA RUSSELL

FLORIDA DREAMS (IRE) 5 b g

A 34,000euros purchase who is related to 2m4f hurdle winner Tara Line, Florida Dreams made his racecourse debut in a Musselburgh bumper in early January where he created a favourable impression by beating a pair of rivals who had already gained experience in Irish points. He beat that pair and his other ten rivals with ease, with Danny McMenamin able to ease him near the finish. The Raceform race reader commented: "He has plenty to recommend him on looks and he looks the type to do well over further when he goes jumping." He was put away until the Grade 2 Aintree bumper in April, a race which often throws up some useful types, and he once again finished with purpose in that 20-runner contest to win by one-and-a-half lengths from the Willie Mullins-trained Blizzard Of Oz. Danny McMenamin was full of praise for his mount: "It was a rough race but Florida Dreams was very tough. He has the speed for this trip (2m 209y) but he stays well and there's plenty of options for him. He's a really nice horse to go hurdling next season." NICKY RICHARDS

GAELIC WARRIOR (GER) 5 b g

Rated only 129 when chinned by Brazil in the 2022 Boodles Juvenile Handicap Hurdle (formerly the Fred Winter), Gaelic Warrior wasn't seen again until December of that year when hosing up in an ordinary maiden hurdle at Tramore, a race which proved that at least he was still fit and healthy. He won another ordinary race at Clonmel over 2m 164y a month later but he faced a much stiffer test when running in a 2m handicap off his new rating of 143 at Leopardstown a few weeks later. He won that competitive contest convincingly despite the burden of top weight and the beaten horses included the likes of

Ballyadam, Anna Bunina and Effernock Fizz. He next ran in the Ballymore Novices' Hurdle at Cheltenham and he finished second at the Festival for the second consecutive year, this time behind stablemate Impaire Et Passe. That was his first try at 2m5f and he did exceptionally well in the circumstances as he got worked up before the start (losing his earplugs on his way to the post) before taking a keen hold in the race itself. His rider Patrick Mullins said afterwards that longer trips would suit the gelding and he proved it on his final start of the season at Punchestown, where he ran away with a Grade 1 over just shy of 3m. He's clearly a top-class staying hurdler in the making but he's built like a chaser and he may be sent over fences this season. If that's the case, a race like the Turners Novices' Chase over just shy of 2m4f could be a viable target – he's currently available at around 12/1 for that contest and perhaps he can make it third time lucky at the festival. WILLIE MULLINS

GALA MARCEAU (FR) 4 b f

The winner of three races in her native France for previous trainer Sylvain Dehez including a Listed contest over 1m7f at Auteuil in April 2022, Gala Marceau joined Willie Mullins in November of that year and she made her debut for him in a Grade 2 Juvenile Hurdle over 2m at Leopardstown on Boxing Day. She finished second of eleven runners behind her stablemate Lossiemouth, finishing well clear of the third, which was a highly encouraging start. Six weeks later she managed to turn the tables on that rival in the Grade 1 Spring Juvenile Hurdle at the Dublin Racing Festival although she was perhaps a shade fortunate as Lossiemouth was hampered at a crucial stage of the contest and by the time she saw daylight the bird had already flown. They met again in the Triumph Hurdle just over a month later and this time Lossiemouth came out on top, although Gala Marceau again ran well to finish second, ahead of Zenta, who would boost the form next time by winning a Grade 1 at Aintree. It became 3-1 to Lossiemouth in the Champion Four-Year-Old Hurdle at Punchestown in April but perhaps Gala Marceau was already in need of a step up in trip by this stage. She saved her best performance until last as she won a Grade 1 over 2m3f 110y at Auteuil in May, with Zarak The Brave, who had finished one place ahead of her at Punchestown, 12l behind her on this occasion. Her trainer was delighted: "We all love a filly who's able to come through a whole season and at the very end put in probably her best performance. Danny (Mullins, rider) thought Gala Marceau would be one who would suit the Mares' Hurdle at Cheltenham next season." That race, over a similar trip to the one she won in France, is therefore the long-term aim and quotes of 12/1 at the time of writing look more than fair. WILLIE MULLINS

GERRI COLOMBE (FR) 7 b g

The winner of seven out of eight races under rules (he also won his sole point start), three of them at Grade 1 level, Gerri Colombe continued his progression last season despite tasting defeat for the first time in his career when just unable to get to The Real Whacker in the Brown Advisory Novices' Chase at the Cheltenham Festival in March – a short head divided them at the finish. Gordon Elliott said afterwards: "Gerri Colombe has been beaten a short-head in a Grade 1 and a stride over the line he is a neck in front, so of course I retain faith in him – he's top class." Despite a hard race at Prestbury Park, he went to Aintree just four weeks later and this time he coasted to victory in the Mildmay Novices' Chase at Aintree over 3m 210y with Elliott sounding far more content afterwards: "We were happy the whole way. Gerri Colombe is a good horse. We were disappointed we got beaten at Cheltenham, I think we were the best horse in the race. That proved it today. He's a horse to look forward to for next year. We'll look to the future now,

Cheltenham is over. You have to dream in this game and he looks to have a whole lot of potential." Presumably the Gold Cup back at Cheltenham will be the primary target for 2023-24, where a rematch with The Real Whacker is a mouthwatering prospect. Throw the likes of Galopin Des Champs and Bravemansgame into the mix and it could be a vintage Gold Cup – Gerri Colombe most certainly deserves his prominence in the betting for that – he's currently available at 8/1. Along the way there will be plenty more Graded races to be won with him provided the ground isn't too quick. GORDON ELLIOTT

GIOVINCO (IRE) 6 b g

A 3m point winner for Michael Griffin at Dromahane last November, Giovinco was sold for £85,000 a month later at the Cheltenham sales and he made his debut for Lucinda Russell in a three-runner novices' hurdle over 2m4f 100y a few months later in March. He won that contest as he liked, catching the eye with some fluent jumps and the Raceform race reader was left in no doubt that he would "go on to better things". Just two weeks later he won another novice hurdle at Carlisle under his penalty by a wide margin, although he wasn't quite as fluent as he had been on his debut. He was stepped up in class for his final assignment in late April, a Listed novices' hurdle over 3m at Perth and he put up by far his most impressive performance, winning by 12l without coming off the bridle. His trainer was ecstatic: "Giovinco is our future, he's a lovely, lovely horse." He apparently goes chasing now and that means connections may plot a similar route to the one trodden by Ahoy Senor a couple of seasons ago – races like the John Francome Novices' Chase at Newbury in December, the Towton Novices' Chase at Wetherby in February and the Brown Advisory Novices' Chase at Cheltenham in March will perhaps be pencilled in for him in what promises to be an exciting season. LUCINDA RUSSELL

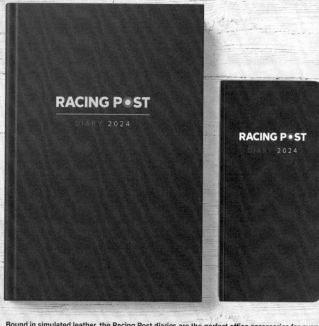

Bound in simulated leather, the Racing Post diaries are the perfect office accessories for every horse racing fan.

Each diary includes all the UK and Irish racing fixtures at the time of publication – jumps, Flat and the all-weather as well as major sporting fixtures, a wealth of racing statistics, principal race dates and details of the racecourses in Britain and Ireland.

The A4 desk diary also includes the principal races and bloodstock sales dates in a week-to-view format along with a racecourse guide, plus a marker-ribbon and gilt edging.

NEW SHOP WEBSITE LIVE NOW!
www.racingpost.com/shop

GO TO WAR (IRE) 5 b g

Fergal O'Brien had his best season as a trainer in 2022-23 with 141 winners and over £160,000 in prize-money. He's now parted company (amicably) with joint-trainer Graeme McPherson so it remains to be seen what impact that will have on his business. However, the early signs so far in the current season have been encouraging and the Irishman looks set for another highly profitable campaign. The trainer has done well with his bumper recruits in recent seasons and he has an exciting jumping prospect in Go To War, who created a good impression in two starts last term. Following a debut win on good ground at Uttoxeter in October (franked by the runner-up, who won next time), he wasn't seen out again until he went to Aintree in April, where he shaped well, finishing eighth of twenty runners behind Florida Dreams, who is also included in these pages. He looked a staying type that day – which is not surprising given he's a half-brother to Flight Deck (who won up to 3m1f) out of a dam who stayed 3m7f so he's unlikely to be seen to best effect until he gets a trip over hurdles. He looks a decent prospect and one who seems sure to win races in that new discipline later this season. FERGAL O'BRIEN

HANDS OF GOLD (IRE) 5 b g

It's still very early days for this fine stamp of a horse who won twice over hurdles last season, but he is clearly going the right way and his shrewd trainer can continue to eke more improvement out of him as he matures. He finished fourth on his debut in a 20-runner maiden hurdle at Down Royal over 2m 190y last November, shaping well and looking like he would benefit from the experience. He then fell early in a similar race over slightly shorter at Thurles the following month but after that he ran fairly well at Limerick (2m) on Boxing Day without ever landing a blow. A month later he was stepped up to 2m4f at Gowran Park and that brought about immediate improvement as he won by 6l from a decent-looking bunch of maidens despite a mistake two out, from which he quickly recovered. Arthur Moore said afterwards: "Hands Of Gold is a grand horse who has been developing mentally and physically. This race was ideal for him. He was a big baby last year, he has an engine and he is going to make a nice chaser." A few weeks later he confirmed the promise of his Gowran win by following up in a novice hurdle over 2m3f at Naas. As he had done on his previous run, he made another fiddly mistake, this time at the third last, but he galloped on resolutely once he recovered from that to win going away. His trainer was considering the Punchestown festival for him with one run beforehand but that plan never materialised after he trailed home in seventh in a handicap over the same C&D as his latest win in March. Again, he made a bad blunder three from home and this time he could not recover. Clearly, there are some jumping issues to iron out but he can only improve on that front and one senses that when he is switched to fences he will perhaps treat his obstacles with a little more respect. In the short-term, there are still races to be won with him over hurdles and he remains a good prospect. ARTHUR MOORE

HARBOUR LAKE (IRE) 7 br g

It's highly likely Harbour Lake's attention will be focused on novice chasing this season. This four-time hurdle winner's form levelled out a bit during the course of last season but he still produced some fine runs including a third place finish in the Greatwood Hurdle at Cheltenham in November and fifth in a competitive Aintree handicap at the National meeting on his most recent outing in April. Although he's yet to race over further than 2m5f, his pedigree is crammed full of stamina being by Shantou out of a Winged Love mare, the dam a sister to 4m National Hunt Chase winner Another Rum, so a step up to 3m should, in theory, be to his liking. He's been a consistent sort so far on ground ranging from good to soft but it shouldn't surprise anyone if this fine, big sort – who is rated 131 over hurdles – takes his form to a new level this time round. ALAN KING

HERMES ALLEN (FR) 6 b g

Much of the talk prior to the 2023 Cheltenham Festival was whether the British trainers would be able to compete with the likes of Willie Mullins, Henry De Bromhead and Gordon Elliott, especially when it came to the novice events. And, although Paul Nicholls won the Turners Novices' Chase with Stage Star, the Somerset trainer's best chance of a winner on the run up to the meeting had looked to be with Hermes Allen in the Ballymore. In fact, he started favourite for that race on the back of hurdle wins at Stratford and Cheltenham in autumn and in the Grade 1 Challow at Newbury on New Year's Eve. That Newbury form had worked out particularly well with seven of the next nine home winning on their next starts and, given the manner in which Hermes Allen disposed of those rivals, it was no surprise to see him start at 9/4 at Cheltenham. He proved disappointing though, racing keenly and dropping away fairly tamely from the last hurdle on ground that may have been soft enough for him. He fared better on less-demanding ground at Aintree on his final start, although he was again below the form of that Challow victory. Hermes Allen has reportedly been given a wind operation over the summer and he's the type that could take his form to a higher level this time round. Whether he stays over hurdles for another season or goes over fences (there is plenty of chase blood in his pedigree) remains to be seen but his presence will enhance whichever category his stable chooses. He should stay 3m when the ground isn't testing. PAUL NICHOLLS

HUGOS NEW HORSE (FR) 6 b g

The Stewart family have been long-standing patrons at
the stable of Paul Nicholls throughout this century, their
best horse undoubtedly Big Buck's, an outstanding staying
hurdler between early 2009 and late 2012. Sadly, Andy
Stewart died at the age of 70 in 2021, but his legacy lives on
and the family have one to look forward to in the coming
months with Hugos New Horse, who won five of his seven
races over hurdles last season. A half-brother to the yard's
high-class chaser Black Corton, he was beaten on his
hurdles debut at Chepstow last October but he went on to
win his next four starts from 2m to 2m4f on a wide array of
surfaces. The winning run came to a halt in a competitive
handicap at Sandown on Imperial Cup day in March where
he finished third behind Crambo and Inneston but that
form could hardly have worked out any better with seven
of the runners, including this 6yo,winning next time. He
was put away after winning his final start at Ayr in April
back in novice company and he's one to look forward to this
season, especially as he goes up further in distance. When
the time comes, he should be equally effective over fences,
but he's very likely to make his mark again in this discipline
before that. PAUL NICHOLLS

IBERICO LORD (FR) 5 b g

It's fair to say that French bumper winner Iberico Lord
wasn't an instant success for Nicky Henderson, although
he was rather pitched in at the proverbial deep end on
his hurdling debut and first run for the yard in a Grade
2 at Cheltenham in November. He dropped away after
a couple of errors in that race won by Fennor Cross,
his fate already sealed when he lost his footing in the
home straight. Better was expected of him over 2m at
Kempton a month-and-a-half later but he was already
back-pedalling when falling at the final hurdle in a race
won by Rare Edition. He was then given a wind operation
and three months off and that seemed to pay dividends

as he turned in a much improved display in a heavy ground Stratford novice event to beat previous scorer Beau Balko by a head, the pair clear of the remainder. On that evidence he looked one to take into handicaps and he proved the point on his final start when finishing a close second (clear of the rest) to stable companion Under Control at Sandown on the final day of the jumps season. There's enough in his pedigree to think he'll be at least as effective as he goes up in distance and this unexposed sort looks sure to win more races in this sphere before he goes chasing. NICKY HENDERSON

IMPAIRE ET PASSE (FR) 5 b g

Before this 155,000euros purchase for 'double green' owners Simon Munir and Isaac Souede ran in the Ballymore Novices' Hurdle at this year's Cheltenham Festival, their racing manager Anthony Bromley was fairly cautious: "It's not to be underestimated that he's only had one bumper run in France and two hurdle races, in the first of which four of the hurdles were bypassed because of low sun, so he's not had a lot of experience going into the cauldron of Cheltenham. I think he's a massive prospect for the years to come, but we'll see how he gets on in what will be only his fourth ever start. He's a scopey horse who will make a lovely chaser and has huge untapped potential. Whether or not he's got enough experience to take this all in, who knows? But he's very exciting." Well, Impaire Et Passe more than lived up to the hype as he won impressively from stablemates Gaelic Warrior and Champ Kiely without ever looking in any danger. Six weeks later he added his second Grade 1 at Punchestown over 2m3f in fairly workmanlike fashion, although Champ Kiely was even further behind him than he had been at Cheltenham. He's built like a chaser so connections now have an interesting decision to make – stay over hurdles for one more season and target the Champion Hurdle, where Constitution Hill and/or Marine Nationale may be lying in wait, or switch to fences straight away and go for the Arkle or the Turners? He's shortest in the ante-post markets for the latter race and that looks the most obvious target if he does go chasing but whatever decision is taken he should be able to retain his unbeaten record for quite a while longer. WILLIE MULLINS

IMPERIAL MERLIN (IRE) 6 b g

This summer Malton trainer John Quinn was in the headlines after a memorable week on the training front at the Goodwood Festival in August, resulting in three winners and a second from five runners. Although mainly Flat-oriented these days, he was a jump jockey before setting up as a trainer and he still has a handful of runners at what was once perceived as "the winter game". So far he's done a good job with Imperial Merlin, who won a bumper in April 2022 and he added three more wins in his four completed starts over hurdles last season, though ironically his best Raceform Rating came on his penultimate outing in February, where he was in the process of running well when falling at the final hurdle at Doncaster. He showed himself none the worse for that experience when returning to winning ways at Ayr on his final start in April, his first run over 3m. Paul Costello, who is involved with the owners (Imperial Racing) said after that win: "We have some good jumps horses and Imperial Merlin is one of them. We were hoping to go to Aintree with him but he fell the last time so we decided to give him a bit of extra time off to come here. He might go straight over fences now but he's got a lot of scope off his mark, probably even when he's put up." Judging by those remarks, all options are still open and he's the type to make further progress. JOHN QUINN

IMPERVIOUS (IRE) 7 b m

This mare went from strength to strength in her first season over fences, remaining unbeaten in five starts including a

trio of Grade 2 races, and there's every reason to believe
that there is even more to come from her this term as she
steps up in trip. She was rated in the 130s over hurdles but
she looked a natural over fences on her first two starts in
late 2022, winning a 2m beginners' chase at Wexford in late
October and then following up in grand style in an above-
average Grade 2 mares' novices chase at Cork (2m 160y) in
mid-December. The horses she beat at Wexford, Dinoblue,
Roseys Hollow and Instit, would all go on to boost the form
subsequently. Impervious was sold by Paul McKeon to JP
McManus in January and the mare started to repay her
purchase price instantly by running out a convincing winner
of a Grade 3 novices' chase at Punchestown over 2m3f 160y,
in which she beat Journey With Me and Minella Crooner
despite meeting those two rivals on 8lb worse terms than
if she had met them in a Grade 1. She then took on the
highly-touted Allegorie De Vassy in the Mares' Chase over
2m4f 127y at the Cheltenham Festival in March and that
race didn't disappoint, with Impervious battling back after
being headed to win by two-and-a-half lengths from her
main market rival. Her final assignment was the Grade 2
Mares' Chase at Punchestown over 2m5f and she won it
convincingly from three Willie Mullins-trained mares –
Instit, Allegorie De Vassy and Elimay. Colm Murphy was
ecstatic: "Impervious has been a revelation and it's amazing
how much she has improved. She can go up or down in trip
and she has loads of options. We can dream away for the
summer." One dream could be the Gold Cup at Cheltenham,
with the 7lb weight allowance she would receive from the
males an added bonus. She will certainly be able to continue
progressing as she steps up further in trip and she's very
much one to keep onside. Unfortunately, Impervious injured
a joint while out cantering in early September and Colm
Murphy said she would be out until after Christmas at the
earliest. Hopefully she makes a full recovery and we can see
her again at all the major festivals in the spring.
COLM MURPHY

INOTHEWAYURTHINKIN (IRE) 5 b g

Gavin Cromwell's gelding created a fine impression when winning a 23-runner maiden hurdle and an eight-runner novice hurdle in November 2022, so much so that he was pitched into Grade 1 company in the Lawlor Of Naas novice hurdle over an extra half mile on his next start in January. He ran a perfectly respectable race, finishing fourth of eight to Champ Kiely, with the promise of further improvement to come. He didn't actually better that effort however, with a drop back to 2m looking against him in a Listed event at Navan the following month. Although he ran well in terms of Raceform Ratings going back up in distance, the 5yo again had his limitations exposed at the highest level at Punchestown on his final start, when fourth to impressive Ballymore winner Impaire Et Passe in the Grade 1 Champion Novice Hurdle (2m 3f). However, he should have learned plenty from that first season of racing and he has scope from a handicapping perspective given he'll start the season on a rating of 137. He's likely to make up into a Listed or minor Graded performer at some point, he should stay 3m, he's effective on anything from yielding to heavy ground and he will also be a decent chaser when the time comes. GAVIN CROMWELL

JOHNNYWHO (IRE) 6 br g

A half-brother to four winners including Doing Fine, Chloe's Court and Howaya Aoife out of a useful mare who finished fourth in the Irish National, Johnnywho won a 3m maiden point at Rathcannon for Ellmarie Holden by 13l in October 2021. A further 6l back in third was Hermes Allen who impressively won the Grade 1 Challow Hurdle last term for Paul Nicholls. Johnnywho was sold to JP McManus after his point win but didn't see the racecourse again for 515 days with what Jonjo O'Neill Jnr described as "loads of small issues at home, nothing major, but just enough to keep him off the track and we just wanted to make sure he was right when we did eventually run him."

That run finally came in a Taunton bumper over 2m and half a furlong in late March which he won at a canter despite being fairly weak in the betting. His rider was happy afterwards, saying: "It probably wasn't the strongest bumper in the world but you would have to like how he did it. We just wanted to get him out on track and we are now nearing the end of the season – we want to keep him as a novice for hurdles next season so I'd imagine we will probably leave him for now and look forward to hurdling next year." His rider thinks that there is plenty of stamina to draw upon so look out for him in novice hurdles at around 3m. The Taunton race was run on soft ground with heavy patches but it is felt that he will be equally at home on faster conditions and he's an exciting prospect for the yard. JONJO O'NEILL

JONBON (FR) 7 b g

Not only is Jonbon still only a 7yo, he's only been beaten twice in his thirteen starts (including a point) – once in the 2022 Supreme Novices' Hurdle behind Constitution Hill and then in last season's Arkle, when he was outpointed by El Fabiolo, who is currently still unbeaten over fences. After his latest Cheltenham defeat there was talk about stepping him up in distance but he stayed over the minimum trip for his final two starts of the season – both Grade 1s – and he won them both so it's still open to debate what route is chosen for him this season. It was a below-par edition of the Maghull Novices' Chase that he won at Aintree in April but he slammed his three rivals by 43l and more without any fuss and, as the saying goes, you can only beat what's put in front of you. Just two weeks later he faced a stiffer task at Sandown in the Celebration Chase but he still proved up to it as he kept on well to see off Captain Guinness, who rates a solid benchmark for the grade. Henderson said afterwards: "My final deciding reason for running was we'd find out if he could take these two-milers on who he'd be meeting next year. If he can cope with them around here, now, then we can start thinking of Tingle Creeks next year – and that's what he's answered." Therefore, it looks like a step up in trip is on hold for the time being but that option remains and it wouldn't be a surprise if we saw him in the Ryanair Chase rather than the Queen Mother at this season's Cheltenham Festival. Whatever the case, he looks sure to notch a few more wins for this publication in the coming months. NICKY HENDERSON

KANSAS DU BERLAIS (FR) 4 gr g

Kansas Du Berlais proved a bit disappointing on his latest start in a competitive 2m handicap hurdle at Sandown on the final day of the last jumps season but, as that was his fifth start since February and his second one in eight days, he may well have been feeling the effects of a busy period. The grey had looked progressive for Gary Moore following a wind operation after his first run for the yard in December and he showed improved form to win over a trip just short of 2m2f on heavy ground at Fontwell in March, staying on strongly in the straight to beat a reliable yardstick in Awaythelad by six lengths, with daylight back to the third home. He followed up back at Fontwell a month later, this time on good ground over a slightly longer distance, beating the 93-rated Tzunami by eighteen lengths, in the process registering his best Raceform Rating. On the back of that he started the 11/2 favourite at Sandown but he offered little in the way of resistance when pressure was applied, though he did keep on a bit again in the closing stages, shaping as though a return to further would be to his liking. A mark of 116 shouldn't prove beyond him in handicaps this time round and he should also stay further than 2m4f. GARY MOORE

KATEIRA 6 b m

A daughter of Kayf Tara and a half-sister to El Presente, a useful staying chaser for Kim Bailey, Kateira made rapid strides in her first season over hurdles and there should be plenty more to come from her as she steps up further in trip. Having finished fifth of twenty in the Grade 2 Mares' Bumper at the Aintree Festival in April of 2022, she got off the mark at the first time of asking over hurdles in a mares' novice over just shy of 2m in November. Despite taking a keen hold and making an early mistake, she proved far too good for her eight rivals, skipping clear from the second last to win by seven-and-a-half lengths from Fay Ce Que Voudras, who franked the form next time by winning a novices' handicap. She was stepped up to 2m4f at Huntingdon for her next assignment in January and she came through that with flying colours despite carrying a 7lb penalty, winning by 13l from another next-time-out-winner Lets Go To Vegas. She was dropped back to 2m 125y at Market Rasen the following month and, despite a 10lb penalty for her earlier wins, she ran out a 19-length winner despite a couple of fiddly errors late in the piece. Again the form was advertised by the runner-up, Shelikesthelights, who won her next two starts. Kateira took on geldings for the first time in the Grade 1 Mersey Novices' Hurdle on her final start in April, but she ran another stormer, finding only Irish Point too good – in behind her were horses like Hermes Allen, You Wear It Well and Springwell Bay. The winner simply got first run on her and she couldn't lay a glove on him despite keeping on well in the closing stages. That run augurs well for her future as she is bred to stay further so expect to see her in some nice handicaps at around 3m. She should also make a lovely staying chaser in time. DAN SKELTON

KILBEG KING (IRE) 8 b g

A point-to-point winner for Colin Bowe at Ballindenisk in the autumn of 2020, Kilbeg King was sold for £45,000 afterwards and he won a 2m bumper at Uttoxeter with plenty in hand on his first start for his new connections in the spring of 2021. Plenty of winners emerged from

that race, including Kilbeg King himself, who won
an ordinary maiden hurdle over 2m4f at Ffos Las in
November after a 595-day absence following a tendon
problem, shaping as though further would suit him in
time. He finished well beaten in the Grade 1 Challow
Hurdle behind Hermes Allen on his next outing on
New Year's Eve but it was an odd race in which they
went a searching gallop, plus it was one that worked out
remarkably well, with next-time-out wins for the second,
fourth, fifth, sixth and two horses that were pulled up.
Back in calmer waters at Fontwell in February, Kilbeg
King ran out an authoritative winner of a novices' hurdle
over 2m5f 164y, and he then ran in a handicap hurdle
over 3m at Newbury in March, where he finished a neck
behind the revitalised On The Blind Side, with 17l back to
the next finisher. He went to the Punchestown festival a
month later where he won a 25-runner handicap hurdle
over 2m7f 130y by four-and-a-half lengths. Anthony
Honeyball said afterwards: "We weren't sure if he was
good enough but we felt that he'd run his race. Aidan
(Coleman) gave him an absolute peach. He had to scrap
a bit to get him out and once he got out he cut loose. He
had quite a hard race at Newbury when finishing second
and we thought we'd wait until Punchestown. I think the
better ground was probably a help although he's a heavy-
topped horse and it wouldn't want to be any quicker than
this." Already an 8yo, chasing will no doubt be on the
agenda sooner rather than later and he looks the type to
do well as a staying novice chaser in the coming months.
ANTHONY HONEYBALL

KILLER KANE (IRE) 8 b g

In his first full season as the named trainer on the licence,
Joe Tizzard sent out 55 winners from nearly 500 runners
over jumps, earning just over £1m in prize money. The
former jockey, who was instrumental in his father Colin's
success over the years, has already been seen to good

effect with the likes of Amarillo Sky and Elixir Du Nutz and he has a healthy blend of quality and quantity in the yard. In Killer Kane Tizzard has one that could prove a bit of a money-spinner this season as he's fine at carrying big weights in some of the lesser handicaps and his current rating should ensure that he's eligible for several of the bigger ones. Although he won only once last season, he took his form to a higher level with that Kempton win over 3m in February, again showing a liking for that course and also for a sound surface, plus the form was franked by the subsequent win of the third. He was a bit below that level in a higher grade next time but he returned to form when third to Bill Baxter in the Topham at Aintree, a combination of the 2m5f trip and the softer ground just finding him out. He'll be suited by a return to a longer trip on less testing ground. JOE TIZZARD

LADYBANK 5 b m

The Kenny Alexander colours (sky blue with white spots on the body) have been a familiar sight in Ireland over the last few years and they were immortalised by Honeysuckle, who racked up sixteen consecutive rules wins between 2018 and last April, including two Champion Hurdles, two Mares' Hurdles and a raft of other victories at the highest level. Although that mare is now retired from racing, Alexander has the likes of Gala Marceau and Halka Du Tabert to look forward to this season and bubbling a bit further down the pecking order is Ladybank, who could be the type to raise her game this time round. Not much was expected from her on debut at Leopardstown at the turn of the year as she started at 100/1 and never figured but she stepped up considerably on that effort when scoring at 40/1 at Punchestown in late January, keeping on well to force a dead-heat with Princess Zoe despite her rider dropping the whip. She was raised in grade and dropped in trip for her final two starts at the Cheltenham and Punchestown Festivals but she never got competitive over those inadequate distances. She'll be suited by a return to 2m4f and, although Listed/Graded success will be the ultimate aim this season, she can't be rated too highly by the handicapper for what she's done so far and the handicap route could be the best option for her early on. HENRY DE BROMHEAD

LETS GO CHAMP (IRE) 8 b g

Despite winning a point on his debut in 2019, Lets Go Champ, who cost current owner Roger Brookhouse £375,000 at Goffs spring horses-in-training sale in May 2022, wasn't seen out under rules until early 2023 at Punchestown, where he shaped with promise to finish third behind Tactical Move over 2m. The step up to 2m3f at Naas brought about improvement on his next start, where he finished second to the Willie Mullins-trained Nick Rockett (who won a Grade 2 on his next start), the pair clear of the rest. Further improvement followed when he scored at Tipperary in April and, although he didn't better that effort in terms of ratings when upped to 3m on his final start at Punchestown, he showed that he had no problem with the longer trip by finishing an excellent second of 25 runners behind Kilbeg King in an ultra-competitive handicap hurdle. Given his relative inexperience and the fact that he's housed in one of the best yards in Ireland, it's reasonable to assume there will be more progress to come and he's likely to win again over hurdles before he embarks on a chasing career. HENRY DE BROMHEAD

LUCKIE SEVEN (IRE) 5 b g

Everything about Luckie Seven's pedigree and what he did in bumpers last season suggests he should make up into a decent hurdler this season. This third foal of a point/2m1f-2m3f hurdle winner ran well first time up at Doncaster in January, staying on nicely in the closing stages to finish a respectable second to Willmount, who

followed up over the same course and distance on his
only subsequent start nearly two months later. Luckie
Seven also reappeared at Doncaster and this time he went
one better on ground just on the easy side of good, with
the third, Destroytheevidence, subsequently winning
over hurdles. But his best effort was reserved for his final
start in a traditionally strong bumper at Ayr on Scottish
National day when he ran the well-backed Charles
Byrnes-trained market leader Bumble Bee Bet to half
a length. He'll be suited by at least 2m4f when he goes
over hurdles this season, although his excellent trainer
will no doubt be taking his time with him. It will also be
interesting to learn whether he handles more extremes
of ground or whether he's best suited to a sound surface.
Whatever the case, he looks sure to win more races.
NICKY RICHARDS

MAGICAL ZOE (IRE) 5 b m

Debut bumper winner Magical Zoe quickly made up into
a smart hurdler last season and she's just the type who
could win further Black Type this time around. Henry De
Bromhead's 5yo justified market confidence in a low-key
Wexford event on her hurdling debut last September,
where she jumped soundly in the main and proved far too
good for a fairly ordinary field. Her trainer obviously holds
her in high regard as she was pitched straight into Grade
3 company only two months later for her next start and
she didn't disappoint, turning in a much-improved display
to beat a field that included several subsequent winners,
including The Model Kingdom and Liberty Dance. Her best
effort came in defeat in the Grade 2 Mares' Novices' Hurdle
at the Cheltenham Festival four months later, where she
finished a fine second to the tough and progressive You
Wear It Well, faring the best of those held up. She was
disappointing on her only other start in a Grade 1 novice
event at Fairyhouse, but, it's as yet unclear whether she
failed to stay the 2m4f trip or whether she hadn't got

over those Cheltenham exertions. There's enough in her pedigree to think she'll stay the longer trip and, if she does, that'll open her options up for the forthcoming season. HENRY DE BROMHEAD

MAHLER MISSION (IRE) 7 b g

Although Mahler Mission only won one of his five starts over fences last season he took his form to a higher level and was arguably unlucky to come away with just that one victory. Given his pedigree and his physique, he looked just the type that would do better over fences than he had over hurdles, although his chase debut proved a disappointing one as he trailed in a well-beaten second at Cheltenham on good ground in October, over 60 lengths behind the Gordon Elliott-trained Chemical Energy. He stepped up considerably on that form at Punchestown 70 days later, where the heavy ground made it much more of a stamina test and he registered another huge chunk of improvement when bolting up in a beginners' chase at Navan in January, beating Tenzing and Gars De Sceaux by 10l and more. He was unlucky to be mugged by Churchstonewarrior in a Grade 2 back at Navan on his next start and even unluckier to fall (he's normally a sound jumper) when holding a clear lead in the National Hunt Chase at the Cheltenham Festival in March, having the field on the stretch from a long way out and still holding a four-length lead when coming down at the penultimate fence. Whether he'd have held on is a topic for discussion but the run showed how far he'd come given that he had Chemical Energy back in third when coming to grief. He's a proper old-fashioned chaser, a real staying type who is well up to winning in Graded company this time round. JOHN McCONNELL

MAKIN'YOURMINDUP 6 b g

Makin'yourmindup, who finished third in a point on his debut in 2021, didn't achieve much in a bumper or on

his first run over hurdles in the 2021-22 season but he made up into a useful hurdler last season, culminating with a win in Grade 2 company at Haydock in February. He stepped up a fair way on the form of his hurdle debut when scoring at Chepstow on his reappearance in October and bettered that effort when upped to 3m at the same course in December. He improved again at Kempton (soft) in January but his best effort came in that Haydock race, where he wasn't altogether fluent but still showed a gritty attitude in the closing stages to land the Grade 2 prize by a short head from Collectors Item. He sidestepped the big spring festivals, reappearing after a two-month break to finish fourth in a Listed event comprising several previous winners at Perth. That effort, while respectable enough, was a shade below the pick of his form but he's only six and very much the type to do better this year – whether that's over hurdles or fences. He's in good hands and looks sure to win more races.
PAUL NICHOLLS

MARINE NATIONALE (IRE) 6 b g

Former stockbroker Barry Connell has been actively involved in racing since his late twenties when he bought his first horse and he has also had spells as an amateur jockey (in his 40s) which included riding winners at Cheltenham's November meeting in 2003, while in 2015 he owned a Cheltenham Festival winner in the shape of Martello Tower, who won the Albert Bartlett for trainer Margaret Mullins. A few years ago Connell took out a training licence himself and he can now boast his first Cheltenham Festival winner, Marine Nationale, who also runs in his colours. The Supreme Novices' Hurdle which this French Navy gelding won in March was a quality edition, with the runner-up Facile Vega and the fourth-placed Inthepocket both winning Grade 1s on their next outings, while the eleventh-placed finisher Fennor Cross won a competitive Grade 3 handicap at Aintree on his

next start. The bullish trainer was delighted afterwards:
"Marine Nationale is unlike any other horse we've had
before – they were mainly stayers, this is a quick horse,
he's probably a Group 1 horse on the Flat, and we might
get around to that at some stage. But today was his day.
He's had five runs and won all five. His jockey (Michael
O'Sullivan) is a superstar. I think we'll come back here for
the Arkle next year. Those are my initial thoughts at this
period in time." Marine Nationale was supposed to run
at Punchestown in April but Connell decided to pull him
out and give him a "proper break", adding: "We're looking
forward to next season and we have all the options
open between the Champion Hurdle route and novice
chasing. We'll leave that decision until he comes back in
again." He's certainly one to look forward to whatever is
decided – if he is aimed at the Champion Hurdle he could
potentially face Constitution Hill and that would be a
clash to savour. BARRY CONNELL

MONBEG GENIUS (IRE) 7 b g

The 2023 Ultima Chase at the Cheltenham Festival was
one of the strongest pieces of handicap form throughout
the entire season. Corach Rambler, who was winning
the race for the second year in succession, went on to
win the Grand National by a wide margin in April while
the runner-up Fastorslow caused an upset in the Grade
1 Punchestown Gold Cup on his next start by beating
Cheltenham Gold Cup winner Galopin Des Champs and
the runner-up there Bravemansgame. Third in the Ultima
was Monbeg Genius, who had won his three previous
starts over fences (all handicaps) and, although his
winning run came to an end, it still represented a career-
best effort. He'd have been an interesting runner in the
Scottish National on the back of that but he was taken
out of that race on account of unsuitable (good) ground.
However, he's just the type to win a top handicap over
3m and beyond this season. The Coral Cup (formerly the

Hennessy) over 3m2f at Newbury in early December – a race his trainer won in 2018 with Cloth Cap – looks a viable early-season target and it wouldn't be a surprise if he made up into a Grand National horse further down the line. He's not fully exposed after only nine rules starts and he is still only seven so there should be a fair bit more improvement to come. JONJO O'NEILL

MONTREGARD (FR) 4 ch g

A half-brother to the high-class staying chaser Protektorat, Montregard caught the eye in a juvenile maiden hurdle over two miles and half a furlong at Doncaster in February, where, having being badly outpaced from the fourth last, he picked up well in the closing stages to finish just over ten lengths behind the winner Sarsons Risk. It looked like the experience would not be lost on him and, given his breeding, a step up in distance was also expected to bring about immediate improvement. His next assignment was a 2m3f maiden hurdle at Warwick in late April, for which he was sent off the 5-6 favourite but he made fairly hard work of justifying those cramped odds as he prevailed by just three-quarters of a length from Democritus. However, he was again outpaced as the race began in earnest before he rallied well from two out and he then fairly motored home to lead at the last. His jumping wasn't flawless at Warwick but it seemed to get better as the race developed and it would appear that he already needs a trip of around 3m. He's been given a BHA rating of 105 and that is a mark he can exploit as he steps up further in trip. TOM LACEY

MYSTICAL POWER (IRE) 4 b g

If ever a horse was bred to do well over jumps it's surely Mystical Power, whose pedigree jumps off the page given he's by outstanding Flat sire Galileo out of top-class hurdler Annie Power. As we all know, there's sometimes a world of difference between what a horse is bred to do and what it actually does but, so far,

Mystical Power hasn't disappointed, winning his only bumper start in workmanlike fashion but proving much more flamboyant when taking the opening race at this season's Galway Festival on his hurdling debut. Despite taking a good hold and proving less than fluent at a few of his obstacles, he travelled with some purpose before easing to the front and pulling clear in the closing stages, prompting his trainer to say: "That was a huge performance when compared to his bumper win. There's a lot of improvement left in his jumping, he made at least three mistakes, maybe four. Hopefully he can be half as good as his mother. We'll continue hurdling with him rather than going back to the Flat, I might do that next year with him. He looks like a horse for maybe the Royal Bond. Mark (Walsh, jockey) pulled him out early as he said he was too keen over the first two flights but I thought he had jumped very well over them. Then he said he was idling a bit past the winning post but once he gave him a squeeze and got him back up into the race he just locked on again. I wouldn't say he showed us any more at home than he had before Ballinrobe but he's just improving with age and maturity. He sweated a lot last time but today he didn't turn a hair. He's coming together nicely." He's entitled to come on a fair bit for that run and he has all the ingredients needed to become a top-class performer. WILLIE MULLINS

NICK ROCKETT (IRE) 6 b g

The winner of a point at Curraghmore for Pat Doyle in late 2021, Nick Rockett made his debut for Willie Mullins in an above-average Fairyhouse bumper in December 2022 in which he acquitted himself well, finishing fourth. Plenty of next-time-out winners came out of that race, including Nick Rockett himself, who improved to win another bumper over just short of 2m at Thurles in February. His hurdles debut came just over a month later over 2m3f at Naas, where he got the better of Lets Go

Champ, a next-time-out winner, in a protracted battle, with twelve other rivals left well behind. He improved again to win his final start of last season, a Fairyhouse novice hurdle over 2m4f 100y by 15l and two of the horses who finished in behind went on to win next time, so the form looks okay. No plans have been mapped out for him but he could win more races over hurdles, perhaps over slightly further, after which he will no doubt be sent chasing. He looks a nice prospect for the yard in that sphere. WILLIE MULLINS

NO ORDINARY JOE (IRE) 7 b g

The winner of three of his first four races in late 2020 and early 2021, No Ordinary Joe ran a cracker when third to West Cork and Adagio in the Greatwood Handicap Hurdle at Cheltenham that November but he was off for just over twelve months with what Nicky Henderson described as "a few little issues" after running disappointingly in another Grade 3 handicap hurdle just before Christmas of that year. He returned with a bang at Kempton on the day after Boxing Day in 2022, winning a competitive 2m handicap hurdle from Big Boy Bobby in a thrilling finish in which he fought back after being headed. He was a bit disappointing in the Betfair Hurdle six weeks later but he put his career back on track with a fine second behind Iroko in the Martin Pipe Handicap Hurdle at Cheltenham, only giving best to a well-handicapped rival in the closing stages. He again ran well when seventh of twenty behind winning machine Fennor Cross in a Grade 3 handicap hurdle over 2m4f at Aintree, where he would have finished closer had it not been for a few untidy jumps. He's now expected to go chasing and, provided he stays healthy, he should have no trouble adding to his tally; his long-term aim could be a race like the Turners Novices' Chase at next year's Cheltenham Festival, which Henderson won in 2021 with Chantry House. NICKY HENDERSON

NOTHINGTOCHANCE 6 b m

A full sister to the Arkle/Tingle Creek winner Edwardstone, Nothingtochance ran in a couple of bumpers in early 2022 before making a fairly inauspicious hurdling debut over 2m at Lingfield in December, where she was never better than mid-division. She was a big eye-catcher two months later at Exeter, however, when she finished a clear second behind the 4/11 winner Bonttay, with subsequent winners filling the next two places. She stayed on stoutly at the Devon track, suggesting that maybe a stiffer test would suit her in time, but she was kept to 2m for her next assignment, which came in a maiden hurdle at Fakenham, where she faced males for the first time. That proved to be no bother to her as she ran out a six-and-a-half-length winner from dual subsequent scorer Lucid Dreams, with a yawning gap back to the rest. A month later she went up to Bangor for a novices' handicap hurdle but she got no further than the second flight, where she stumbled an unseated Tom Cannon. It was just plain bad luck on her part rather than exposing any jumping flaws so she can easily be forgiven for that. She can resume her progress over hurdles this autumn, with a mark of 114 certainly not looking too harsh given that Edwardstone went on to be rated 150 over hurdles and he is currently rated 169 over fences. She probably won't end up being as good as him of course, but there is still plenty of potential upside. ALAN KING

PETIT TONNERRE (FR) 5 b g

A dual winner in his native France in 2021 before winning a three-runner handicap hurdle over 2m 125y at Market Rasen on his first start for Jonjo O'Neill in February of 2022, Petit Tonnerre had some tough assignments in handicaps during the course of last season but he acquitted himself admirably on each occasion and there's every chance that he can win one or two of them this time around. He belied odds of 22/1 when finishing third of eleven in a Class 2 event over

2m4f at Aintree in late October, where he was noted as travelling strongly and keeping on willingly. A month later he ran in a similar contest at Newbury over 2m4f 110y and he again performed with great credit, finishing second to Red Risk with the rest well beaten off. A line can be drawn through his run in the Lanzarote Hurdle at Kempton in January as he was badly hampered and almost knocked over by a faller at the second flight and he was wisely pulled up soon afterwards. He avoided any such mishaps at Ascot in February, where he ran another creditable race by finishing fifth behind Irish Hill, Zoffany Bay and Sammarive over 2m 3f. His final assignment was over 2m 179y at Cheltenham in the County Hurdle and he ran another sound race, finishing seventh of the 24 runners behind Faivoir, having travelled nicely for a long way. That was just his seventh run in this country and his tenth overall and there's every chance that there's more to come from him as he gains further experience. His rating of 139 is no gimme but he's likely to be aimed at some decent handicaps at around 2m4f this time around and there's certainly a big pot in him. Another tilt at the Lanzarote Hurdle in January and maybe the Coral Cup over 2m5f at next year's Cheltenham Festival in March look like feasible targets. JONJO O'NEILL

RIGHTSOTOM (GER) 4 b g

A son of Maxios with a middle-distance Flat pedigree, Rightsotom finished a clear second of fourteen behind Zarak The Brave in a 2m maiden hurdle at Fairyhouse on his racecourse debut last November. The winner would go on to advertise the form a few times, notably when winning the Grade 3 Galway Hurdle in August of this year. It was a reflection of the esteem in which Rightsotom was held to see him line up in the Triumph Hurdle on his next start in March and he ran far better than his SP of 200/1 would suggest, finishing sixth of the fifteen runners behind Lossiemouth, albeit without ever

**Firsts, Lasts & Onlys: Horse Racing
Truly Wonderful Collection of Horse
Racing Trivia is** filled with improbal
facts and mind-boggling trivia that
will test and tease every horse racin
enthusiast.

Try these questions for size: How did
the word 'thoroughbred' come into
existence, and what is a dam sire?
Which Grand National-winning horse
opened supermarkets after he retire
and was sent requests for autograph
Which BBC sports commentator ofter
had bad luck around the time of the
National? Which classic race almost
came to be known as the Bunbury?

The perfect gift for every horse racin
fan, this is a book you can pick up
while waiting for the stewards' inquir
for the 3.15 at Newmarket and learn
something new, weird or fascinating.
Often all three.

seriously threatening. He ran another good race when finishing fourth behind Zenta in another Grade 1, the 4-Y-O Juvenile Hurdle at Aintree a month later, with the Raceform race reader describing him as "one of the best maiden hurdlers about". He soon shed that tag at Cork, however, when winning an 18-runner maiden hurdle in early May in the manner of a good horse. His jumping was excellent which was noted by trainer Tom Mullins afterwards: "Rightsotom was only having his fourth run, his jumping is deadly. He put it all together today. We will try and pick up another hurdle with him, he could go the Flat route too." He's likely to be targeted at some top handicap hurdles at around 2m this season and he doesn't appear to have any ground preferences, so he's very much one to look forward to as he gains further experience. TOM MULLINS

ROBERT JOHNSON 5 ch g

Given his exploits on the Flat this year, progressive stayer Robert Johnson could return to the jumping game as one of the best handicapped hurdlers in training. The 5yo returned to the Flat and to turf in April rated 54 and he now resides on a mark of 83, having won at Catterick, Thirsk (twice), Musselburgh and York. But his best effort came in defeat in the 2m4f event at Goodwood where, along with Temporize, he pulled clear of the rest in the closing stages, going down a length and a quarter at the line. There may be further challenges ahead on the Flat but when he does go back over hurdles, it'll be from a basement mark of 89, only 6lb above his Flat mark, meaning he could do some damage in ordinary handicaps before the handicapper catches up with him – assuming he can translate that improvement back to this discipline. There's no reason why that shouldn't be the case given his last run over hurdles came prior to his winning spree and that he's not fully exposed in this sphere. PHIL KIRBY

ROCCO ROYALE (IRE) 5 b g

From the same family as classy staying chasers Simon and Freewheelin' Dylan, Rocco Royale was kept to around 2m for his first three starts in late 2022 and early 2023 and he gave the distinct impression on each occasion that he would benefit from a much stiffer test. He made his debut in a strong Worcester bumper in October, where he finished sixth of fourteen behind Roger Pol, another of the hundred, where he was noted as staying on late. He again did all his best work in the closing stages when a keeping-on fifth of eighteen in a 1m7f novices' hurdle on his hurdle debut at Wincanton in February, where he outran odds of 66/1. He was sent off a much shorter price at Ludlow over half a furlong further later the same month but again he was caught flat-footed by a bunch of speedier rivals before making relentless headway from the second last flight to finish third of the fifteen runners behind Welsh Charger and Estacas. That race worked out well with all of the first four home winning one of their next two starts. Rocco Royale was finally stepped up to 2m3f on his final start of the season at Fontwell in early April and this time he proved up to the task, always travelling best and winning cosily under a hands-and-heels ride from Jonjo O'Neill Jr. The Raceform racereader noted afterwards: "He's bred to get a bit further and a more galloping track ought to bring about further improvement." JONJO O'NEILL

ROGER POL (IRE) 5 b g

A half-brother to Adrrastos, the winner of seven races for Jamie Snowden between 2017 and 2019, Roger Pol ran in four bumpers last term, winning twice. He made his debut at Worcester in October where he ran out a fairly comfortable winner of a 2m contest, having been well backed beforehand. The form worked out nicely with the second, third, fourth and sixth all winning races subsequently. Roger Pol was next pitched into a Listed

bumper at Cheltenham in November, but he raced quite keenly there and quickly lost his position over 5f out to trail in ninth behind Gentle Slopes. Back in calmer waters at Ffos Las in January, he ran a good race behind Sole Solution and Norman Fletcher under a penalty in a strong-looking contest for the track. The winner wasn't seen again but the next three home all won their next outing. Roger Pol's final assignment came at Huntingdon two months later where he again justified good market support by ultimately running out a clear winner from Taras Hall despite having to be pushed and shoved along by his rider for much of the contest. Snowden said afterwards: "He's not very big but makes up in heart what he lacks in stature." He was put away for a hurdling campaign in the autumn and he is one to look forward to in that discipline with his trainer saying: "He jumps like an absolute bunny and he should have a really nice future." JAMIE SNOWDEN

RUBAUD (FR) 5 b g

Big things are expected this season from Rubaud, who made up into a very useful performer over hurdles in the latest season. He won four of his six races (all when making over 2m on good ground) under the tutelage of Paul Nicholls, his only defeats coming on soft ground at Kempton in December and when disappointing in the Betfair Hurdle at Newbury in February, where he raced too keenly to do himself justice. He sidestepped the big festivals at Cheltenham and Aintree, his trainer going on record after his Ayr April win to say: "Rubaud had been a bit keen earlier in the season but we still thought we'd try to ride him positively. He's been improving all the time, it was the best thing I ever did not running him at Aintree on the soft ground. He'll be some two-mile chaser next season, I can't wait." Given that ground dependency, he may not be slogging around on soft and heavy ground during the core winter season but he could easily come into his own in the latter months of 2023 and when the ground normally dries out in spring and he'll be a fascinating recruit to the chasing ranks. PAUL NICHOLLS

RUSSIAN RULER (IRE) 6 b g

This steadily progressive gelding overcame a few blips in the winter months before things finally clicked into place for him in spring. Having shaped encouragingly over 2m4f in a race that threw up winners on his reappearance at Newbury in November, Russian Ruler was pulled up over a similar trip at Chepstow a month later and he took a heavy-looking fall (he was in the process of running creditably at the time) back at Newbury over 2m in February. Following a short break, he kept on well to notch his first hurdle win (again at Newbury) over 2m on his handicap debut in March and he followed up a month later at Kempton over the same trip back in novice company, beating Charlie Longsdon's Alien Storm by just under three lengths. His mark remained unchanged on 127 after that victory and he should be able to win again. However, given the chase blood in his pedigree he should improve further once he gets to jump a fence.
NICKY HENDERSON

SAINT DAVY (FR) 6 b g

Following an eight-length win on his debut in an Irish point in November 2021 Saint Davy sold for the eye-watering figure of £270,000 at Goffs a few weeks later but he wasn't seen again until lining up in a Carlisle bumper on his rules debut eleven months later. Despite the modest gallop, he created a favourable impression, leading in the straight and going clear in the closing stages to win in the manner of one who could be capable of better. He was switched to hurdles and upped in trip for his next start at Chepstow and he duly followed up – albeit narrowly – beating Hymac, a Harry Fry-trained bumper winner, by a nose, the pair a long way clear of the remainder. A further step up in trip and the jump up to Grade 1 company found him out on his final start at Aintree in April, where he trailed in ninth of the fifteen runners in a race won by Apple Away which contained a stack of winners. He'll likely be seen to better effect this season and he can win again over hurdles before he gets the chance to tackle fences (there's plenty of chase blood in his pedigree). JONJO O'NEILL

SALVADOR ZIGGY (IRE) 7 b g

Having won a bumper for his previous trainer James Andrew Fahey in September 2021, Salvador Ziggy was sent to Gordon Elliott in May 2022 and he quickly settled into his new surroundings, reeling off a four-timer over hurdles in the next four months over trips ranging from 2m3f 130y to 3m. He then ran well in a Pertemps qualifier on his handicap debut at Cheltenham in October and wasn't seen again until the final at the same venue in March, in which he finished an excellent second of 23 runners behind Good Time Jonny. The Raceform race reader described him as "much more of a chaser on looks" with Gordon Elliott adding: "I'm hopeful a switch to chasing will be the making of him next season." We saw him one more time over hurdles in a Grade 1 over 3m at the end of April but he ran poorly behind Gaelic Warrior, eventually being pulled up having quickly lost his position after two out. However, just six weeks later he made his chasing debut over 3m at the same track and he won impressively, despite a few novicey jumps. Five-and-a-half lengths behind him in second was Hubrisko, who rates a solid yardstick, and the rest were left trailing in his wake. His rider Danny Gilligan said afterwards: "Salvador Ziggy will come on plenty in his jumping. I tried to teach him a bit and he was clever when he got in tight. There will be plenty more days in him." Jack Kennedy rode Salvador Ziggy when he comfortably won two more chases in August at Tramore (2m5f 160y) and

Killarney (2m7f), in the latter of them beating the 140-rate Toss Again as he liked. If he continues progressing, another trip to Cheltenham can be pencilled in for him in March, possibly in the National Hunt Chase over just shy of 4m, for which he is currently available at around 12/1.
GORDON ELLIOTT

SANDOR CLEGANE (IRE) 6 b g
Named after a skilled warrior in the internationally-acclaimed *Game Of Thrones* series, bumper winner Sandor Clegane made up into a smart performer over hurdles in his first season jumping. Although he was turned over on his hurdles debut over 2m at Galway in October, he appreciated the step up to 2m5f on his next outing and showed much-improved form to win a Punchestown maiden by twelve lengths, and that was a race which threw up its fair share of winners. Connections wasted no time in stepping him up in grade and he posted a solid third behind Good Land in a Grade 1 over 2m6f at the Dublin Festival before finishing a fine third again in the Albert Bartlett Novices' Hurdle behind Stay Away Fay and Affordable Fury. He didn't have to match that effort when winning at Punchestown on his final start but he did all that was asked of him in beating the now 127 rated Della Casa Luna in workmanlike fashion back in distance. He'll presumably be going over fences this season and there's every chance he could develop into a top-class performer at around 3m in that sphere given his progressive nature, his pedigree and the fact that he's a fine, strong individual with plenty of physical scope. He's a really exciting prospect.
PAUL NOLAN

SENIOR CHIEF 6 b g
Senior Chief has yet to contest a handicap or a Graded race but he looks the type to win races at either level in the coming season. Following a promising bumper run in a race that threw up winners on his debut in April

2022, he took well to his new discipline last season, with maiden and novice wins at Punchestown (2m4f, yielding) and Navan (2m6f, heavy) in February and March respectively. Following the Navan victory, his trainer said: "Senior Chief is a lovely horse. I like the way he ground it out there. He's still a baby and improving all the time. He qualifies for the Red Mills final at Punchestown and that's where we will probably go." He did tackle the Red Mills and, although he was beaten by Sandor Clegane (also included in these pages), he matched his previous best effort in defeat. There's more than enough in his pedigree and the way he has been shaping to suggest that he'll be suited by the step up to 3m and, similarly, there's enough chase blood in his pedigree to think that he'll do at least as well once he goes over fences. He's still unexposed and ranks as a decent prospect. HENRY DE BROMHEAD

SOME SCOPE 5 b g

Former jockey and Gloucester-based trainer Richard Hobson has already shown what he can do when he gets the right type of animal and he's got one to keep an eye on this season in the shape of Some Scope, who should do better once he gets the chance to tackle fences. The second foal of a point winner with plenty of stamina in his pedigree, Some Scope turned in easily his best effort over hurdles when upped markedly in distance for his handicap debut at Haydock in April, where he stayed on far too strongly for some ordinary rivals over 3m. That form has taken a few knocks – including when Some Scope pulled up at Market Rasen a month later – but he should improve for another summer on his back and he's just the type to win again once he is sent over fences in ordinary handicap company. His trainer confirmed after his Haydock win: "Some Scope is bred to stay and he's a nice horse who'll go chasing next season." He's only raced on good to soft and soft ground so far and he'll likely stay further than 3m in time. RICHARD HOBSON

SONIGINO (FR) 6 b g

A dual hurdles winner for David Cottin in France in the first half of 2021, Sonigino was bought by the syndicate that includes Sir Alex Ferguson and Jed Mason later that year and sent to Paul Nicholls. Already rated 127 at the end of 2021, he took a while to acclimatise to his new surroundings, with five midfield finishes in his first five starts between November 2021 and March 2022, a feature of which was his failure to settle. He was given wind surgery in April of 2022 and that procedure brought about instant improvement – he won on his first start afterwards at Chepstow (2m) in early October and he quickly followed up over the same C&D at the end of the same month. Raised 14lb for those two wins, he was then pitched into the Greatwood Handicap Hurdle at Cheltenham in mid-November but he could only finish eighth behind I Like To Move It, where he perhaps paid the price for trying to serve it up to the eventual winner a long way out. He was given a break after that and, back in calmer waters in February, he resumed the winning thread in a handicap hurdle over 2m3f 137y at Huntingdon, showing a good attitude to see off two persistent challengers in the closing stages. Upped in grade again on his final start of the campaign, he acquitted himself admirably behind Fennor Cross and Buddy One in a 2m4f Grade 3 hurdle at the Aintree Festival, where he stayed on well from an unpromising position to finish on the heels of those two progressive Irish novices. The front three pulled clear and the form stacks up well. A fast-run race suits this gelding ideally and he looks more than capable of winning more races over hurdles. However, chasing is the long-term aim with rider Harry Cobden saying after his win in February: "Whatever Sonigino does over hurdles is a stepping stone to fences." PAUL NICHOLLS

SPRINGWELL BAY 6 b g

Springwell Bay's first season over hurdles was a productive one with three wins from five starts and there's definitely the promise of more to come this term. This bumper winner, who was picked up for his current team for 155,000euros following his debut in 2021, was off for almost eleven months afterwards and he didn't have to match his bumper form to justify prohibitive odds on his hurdles debut at Carlisle in October 2022. Although he was beaten in a Grade 2 at Cheltenham on his next start, he fared a good deal better in terms of form, occupying third place behind Fennor Cross, who went on to win a Grade 3 handicap at Aintree in spring. Further novice wins followed at Ascot and Wetherby (both races at around 2m3f) and, although he was beaten, he ran as well as he ever had done on his final start in a strong Grade 1 at Aintree where he finished sixth behind Irish Point. His trainer said after his Wetherby win that he was in no rush to get him up to 3m as he has been fairly keen but there are plenty more races to be won with him and there's more than enough in his pedigree to suggest he'll be at least as good when he goes over fences. JONJO O'NEILL

STATE MAN (FR) 6 ch g

When the 141-rated State Man won the County Hurdle on his handicap debut at Cheltenham in 2022 only his most ardent supporters would have predicted that he would go on to win five Grade 1s on his next six starts, but that is what he managed to do over the next 13 months – and it would have been six out of six had he not bumped into Constitution Hill in last season's Champion Hurdle. He finished second in that contest, beaten by about 9l, but if you take out the exceptional winner he would have won it comfortably from Zanahyir and Vauban. He did go on to confirm the form with some of those other beaten horses in the following month's Paddy Power Champion Hurdle at Punchestown, in which he made all, after which Willie Mullins said: "Paul just kept it simple, he just missed the last but he fiddled it and

that's what you like to see a hurdler doing. We'll get him back doing the same next season we hope." That's an interesting quote as a few observers have suggested that a switch to fences is on the cards in order to avoid another clash with Constitution Hill. He's currently a best-priced 10/1 for this season's Arkle and 16/1 for the Turners Novices' Chase over half a mile further, but he's also still an 8/1 shot for the Champion Hurdle, which would mean another clash with Constitution Hill, who is staying over hurdles for another season at least. Whatever path is chosen for him, he's only six, he's a class act and he looks more than capable of winning plenty more races.
WILLIE MULLINS

STRONG LEADER 6 b g

It's an indication of the strength in depth among the ranks of the Irish novices that Strong Leader fared the best of the British-trained runners in the most recent running of the Supreme Novices' Hurdle at Cheltenham in March. Despite finishing only ninth, that run – he finished less than thirteen lengths behind the winner Marine Nationale – represented his best one in terms of form to that point and the effort can be upgraded as he is probably most effective on less testing ground. The 6yo, who won his first three starts over hurdles on no worse than good to soft ground between November and January, continued on the upgrade when finishing runner-up on his final start in a Grade 1 at Aintree over 2m, finishing much closer to Henry de Bromhead's winner Inthepocket than he had done at the Cheltenham Festival. Judging by his physique and his pedigree – his dam is an unraced half-sister to high-class staying chaser Strong Flow – it wouldn't be a surprise to see Strong Leader going novice chasing this season and he has all the ingredients needed to make his mark in better company assuming the ground isn't too testing. He should also stay a fair bit further than 2m. OLLY MURPHY

SUPREME GIFT (IRE) 6 b g

There are perhaps two ways of looking at Supreme Gift's form before you decide whether he's a horse to follow or not. On the one hand a glance at his Newcastle December run when he went crashing through the rail and running out at the end of the back straight, coupled with a tailed-off run when upped to 3m in a Grade 2 at Haydock in February, should perhaps sound a note of caution. However, it's probably best to judge him on his other four efforts over hurdles, which saw him register three wins, all at around 2m4f, and a career-best effort when fourth at Cheltenham over that trip on his handicap debut in April. That last piece of form looks fairly strong too, with the winner, Willaston, going on to score next time, as did the horses who finished sixth (chase) and ninth. Although he didn't appear to stay 3m at Haydock, Supreme Gift's pedigree suggests that he'll be worth another try over it, especially when he gets to run in handicaps. He handles good and softer ground and a current mark of 126 is an exploitable one. HENRY DALY

TAHMURAS (FR) 6 b g

A 3m point winner in May 2021, Tahmuras has always looked like a chaser in the making, so the fact that he was able to win four races over hurdles, including a Grade 1, augurs well as he starts jumping those larger obstacles this autumn. The game winner of a strong-looking Wincanton bumper in March 2022, he was sent off as the 11/8 favourite for a maiden hurdle at Chepstow eight months later and he readily justified those odds by running out an eight-length winner. The fourth, sixth, seventh and ninth would all win next time out and plenty of other winners emerged from the race so the form looks rock-solid. Tahmuras was upped to Listed company on his next start at Haydock nearly three weeks later and he took it in his stride, running out a comfortable winner from four rivals who had all won

their previous start. Next came the Tolworth Hurdle at
Sandown in January and that race also set up perfectly
for him, with his stamina being brought into play on the
rain-softened ground. He was always doing enough to
hold off L'Astroboy and Nemean Lion and, once again,
the form was franked with the third, fourth, fifth and
sixth all winning their next outing. The Supreme Novices'
Hurdle proved a different ball game altogether and he
was readily outpaced by the principals in that, eventually
trailing home tenth of the thirteen finishers behind
Marine Nationale. He also came up short at Aintree the
following month in the Grade 1 Top Novices' Hurdle but
a 2m contest on good to soft ground is far from his cup
of tea so he can easily be forgiven that run. Described by
syndicate manager Noel Fehily as "a proper winter horse",
he will now go novice chasing. He may be kept to around
2m in the early part of the season, especially on ground
with plenty of dig, but he may prove best over slightly
further as the season progresses and he's one to bear in
mind for the Turners Novices' Chase over 2m4f, which
Paul Nicholls won this year with Stage Star. Quotes of
50/1 at the time of writing may well underestimate him.
PAUL NICHOLLS

TELECON 6 br g

Apart from one below-par run in Listed company on
just his second outing over hurdles, Telecon's first
season in his new discipline was otherwise one of
steady progression. Having demonstrated ability at an
ordinary level in bumpers, he improved to beat Ladiam,
a subsequent winner, on his hurdles debut over 2m1f
at Ballinrobe last July. His Listed defeat came only one
week later, so there are perhaps valid excuses for that
below-par showing and, although he ran well in terms of
form, he perhaps didn't see out the 2m4f trip as well as
the principals when finishing fourth behind Lieutenant
Highway at Bellewstown in August. He wasn't seen out

again over jumps (though he won a Charity Race on the Flat at the Curragh in September) until April, where he showed improved form to win a 19-runner contest at Fairyhouse when returned to 2m. He then at least matched that effort in a Punchestown handicap just over a fortnight later, where he finished fourth of eighteen over 2m 100y, in a race won by Bialystok which threw up quite a few winners. He can lead or sit handy and he should be able to make his mark in handicap company this time round. MARK FAHEY

THE CARPENTER (IRE) 7 gr g

Second behind the now 134-rated hurdler Gatsby Grey in a 2m Navan bumper for Stuart Crawford in March 2021, The Carpenter was sold privately for an undisclosed fee at the end of that year and he made his belated return to action for his new connections at Exeter in February of this year. He got the better of odds-on favourite Off To A Flyer in that 2m2f 110y novices' hurdle, with his stamina kicking in in the closing stages to win going away. Both the runner-up and the third, who was a distance behind the front pair, would go on to win handicaps subsequently, so the form has a solid look to it. The Carpenter was next seen at Newbury six weeks later and this time he ran out a convincing winner of another novice hurdle over 2m4f 118y, with a couple of last-time-out winners filling the places. He was given a BHA rating of 129 after that win but he was able to make light of it on his handicap debut over 2m4f at Uttoxeter in early May, which he won in uncomplicated fashion. He was put up 5lb but he looks capable of defying that higher mark, especially as he steps up further in trip. A grand stamp of a horse, he's a half-brother to 3m hurdle winner Dubai Angel, who has also won a handicap chase over 2m6f for Dr Richard Newland. Chasing will no doubt be on the agenda sooner or later and he is one to look forward to in that sphere. NICKY HENDERSON

THE CHANGING MAN (IRE) 6 b g

When this gelding won a handicap hurdle over 2m6f at
Stratford in March 2022, the Raceform race reader said:
"He gives the impression that anything he achieves before
going chasing is a bonus." Well, he achieved plenty over the
next twelve months, winning twice more, finishing second
four times and running a sound race when finishing eighth
of 23 in the Pertemps Final at the Cheltenham Festival.
His two wins came at Ffos Las (2m4f) in October and at
Uttoxeter (2m7f) in November and he should also have
won next time at Taunton (3m) in December but he
faltered on the run to the line to finish half a length behind
Apple Rock after hitting the last flight. He improved
on that performance on ratings when finishing runner-
up behind Itchy Feet over 3m1f at Huntingdon in late
January and his second behind Johnson's Blue at Haydock
in February at least matched that level of performance.
His staying-on eighth in the Pertemps Final was followed
by another second place behind Tiger Jet over 3m at
Haydock in April, but it was his best performance to date
based on the Raceform Rating he achieved and the form
has begun to work out well with subsequent wins for the
third, fourth, ninth and eleventh. The 6yo will now turn
his attention to chasing and he looks the type to run up
a sequence over trips of around 3m in the first half of
the season before establishing himself as a handicapper
thereafter. JOE TIZZARD

THE GOFFER (IRE) 6 b g

As mentioned elsewhere in these pages, the latest
running of the Ultima Handicap Chase at Cheltenham
is one of the strongest pieces of handicap form from last
season. The Goffer, who finished fourth, is fancied to
win a decent handicap this season, even though he failed
to figure in this season's Galway Plate in July (he ran as
though that run was just needed following a three-month
break). But, back to the beginning of last season. Gordon

Elliott's gelding put an inauspicious chase debut behind him when scoring over 2m6f at Thurles in November, beating future Grade 2 winner Churchstonewarrior in the process. He added to his tally three runs later on his handicap debut over fences at the Dublin Festival but, although his effort flattened out late, his best run in terms of ratings came in the Ultima. He was kept busy afterwards, running in both the Irish National and the bet365 Gold Cup at Sandown and he ran very well in the latter race, finishing fourth of sixteen runners behind Eider/Scottish National winner Kitty's Light. He's fairly experienced over fences for one of his age and, given he's back to a reasonable mark, he should be able to pick up a decent pot at some stage this season. GORDON ELLIOTT

THE REAL WHACKER (IRE) 7 b g

One of the best races of the 2023 Cheltenham Festival was the Brown Advisory Novices' Chase over 3m in which The Real Whacker and Gerri Colombe fought out a thrilling finish with the former prevailing by just a short head. It meant that the 7yo son of Mahler retained his unbeaten record over fences and, in the process, he inflicted the first and so far only defeat on his rival, who would go on to take his third Grade 1 over fences in the Mildmay Novices' Chase a few weeks later. Patrick Neville, who is the former assistant to Ann Duffield, made no secret of the esteem in which he held his charge after his victory: "I was toying with the Gold Cup this year but we made the decision to try to give The Real Whacker a bit more experience and mind him with the view to coming back next year. We'll give him a good summer as he might have done enough now for this year. He'll probably go to Listowel in the autumn because it's one of my favourite tracks." The race Neville will no doubt target at Listowel is the Kerry National in late September and thereafter all roads will lead back to

Cheltenham for the Gold Cup, with another race or two in between. He's prominent in the betting for the Coral Gold Cup at Newbury at the time of writing but a mark of 162 would mean he'd have to match the likes of Denman, who won his first Hennessy (the former name for that race) when rated 161 in 2007, eight months after winning the Royal & Sun Alliance Chase (the old name for the Brown Advisory Novices' Chase). PATRICK NEVILLE

TRELAWNE 7 b g

Out of a 3m1f chase winner for Kim Bailey in 2007, Trelawne got his career off to the perfect start in February 2022 when running out a wide-margin winner of a 2m2f 111y novice hurdle at Exeter. In behind were future handicap chase winners Triple Trade and Doctor Ken, so it wasn't a weak race by any means. A month later he ran over 2m7f at the same track but he could only finish third of four, although that finishing position doesn't tell the whole story as he was in the process of making his challenge on the run-in when sharply veering off to his left, which presumably was down to greenness. He returned to the track at Ffos Las in November and this time he showed no wayward tendencies as he ran out a game winner of a 2m6f handicap hurdle. It perhaps wasn't the strongest race of its type but he showed a good attitude over a trip which was possibly on the short side for him. He was stepped up to 2m7f at Uttoxeter in March and he made light of his 6lb rise as he ran out a ready winner of a thirteen-runner handicap. He was given a BHA rating of 136 after that race and he looks capable of adding to his tally over hurdles off that mark, especially as he steps up further in trip. In the long term, he looks an exciting prospect for chasing, provided the ground isn't too quick; so far he has only raced on soft. Matt Nicholls, who is Kim Bailey's assistant, said after the gelding's win in March: "Trelawne could be a bit special. He needs soft ground and we've missed most of the winter because of that. He bolted up at Exeter on his debut for us and we've always liked him." KIM BAILEY

TULLYHILL (FR) 5 gr g

Bought for £220,000 after winning a point-to-point at Moira in the autumn of 2022, Tullyhill triumphed on his debut for Willie Mullins in a 2m2f bumper at Gowran Park in March, with Will Do, a next-time-out winner for Gordon Elliott, beaten into second by an easy three-and-a-quarter lengths; there were a further sixteen lengths back to the third horse. Following that victory, Tullyhill was dropped back to two miles at the Punchestown Festival and he ran a great race to finish second behind A Dream to Share, who was completing a rare five-timer, in the Grade 1 bumper. He cruised effortlessly into contention in that event only to be outpointed in the latter stages by a horse with a slightly better turn of foot and a good deal more experience. Looking forward to his hurdling career, the 2m5f trip of the Ballymore Novices' Hurdle should suit Tullyhill ideally and he looks a fair ante-post bet at 12/1 to emerge victorious in that contest at the 2024 Cheltenham Festival. WILLIE MULLINS

TWINJETS (IRE) 6 b g

A dual bumper winner in the first half of 2022, Twinjets ran six times over hurdles last season, winning three. He was a shade disappointing first time up at Cheltenham in October when sent off favourite for a 2m maiden hurdle, in which he finished sixth behind Fennor Cross having been inconvenienced by fallers a couple of times. He was then found a lesser opening over just short of 2m at Leicester in early December and he converted it in straightforward fashion, with the next three home all winning subsequently to give the form a solid look. It was a similar story at Plumpton in January, this time over 2m4f 114y, where he was sent off the 1/3 favourite of a novice hurdle. He won that readily with the step up in trip appearing to suit him well. The winning margin was 9l but the runner-up, Twin Power turned that form around at Sandown next time, by beating Twinjets by 1¾l over just short of 2m4f. It wasn't just the extra 8lbs that he was conceding to his old rival, it may also have been the distance because he already looked in need of a step up to around 3m as he struggled to reel in the Paul Nicholls-trained runner. He next ran in the Grade 1 EBF Final over the same C&D on heavy ground in March but he made no impression in that race which was won by Crambo, and he was pulled up sharply before the last when already well beaten. He bounced back to form in calmer waters at Kempton (2m5f) in April, winning easily despite a 7lb penalty. It was a productive season over hurdles but he's built like a chaser and surely he can win more races in that discipline this coming season. MILTON HARRIS

UNDER CONTROL (FR) 4 ch f

Under Control's career record reads four wins from five starts, with her only defeat coming in the Grade 2 Mares' Novices' Hurdle at the Cheltenham Festival on just her second start for Nicky Henderson. Prior to that well-beaten effort she'd won her only start in France (2m3f, hurdles debut) and she also justified favouritism on her debut at Newbury for her current yard in early March, a run that prompted Henderson to say that he wasn't certain that the Cheltenham Festival a fortnight later would be on the agenda. It was, and when she returned to Prestbury Park in April she got back to winning ways in a Grade 3 handicap, form which has already been franked by subsequent wins for the third and the ninth. Her final start at Sandown resulted in another improved effort, this time getting the better of the stable companion Iberico Lord over 2m. Following that victory, Henderson stated: "Under Control is a sweet little thing. We've only had her for a short time. She's not very big but has grown in stature the whole way through. It was a big ask to do that after running at Cheltenham. We were worried she wouldn't go in the ground today. She's never stopped improving." Given her size it's unlikely she'll be asked to go over fences in the coming season, but there may still be some handicapping scope over hurdles from her current mark. NICKY HENDERSON

WALK AWAY HARRY (IRE) 5 b g

A brother to 3m hurdle winner Spitfire Girl and a half-brother to three more winners at around 2m4f, Walk Away Harry caught the eye in a Clonmel bumper over 2m121y in early April, as he finished strongly from off the pace to force a dead-heat for second behind clear winner Shannon Royale. Eight lengths further back in fourth was Extrapolation who won a bumper by 10l on his next start and he's also won a maiden hurdle subsequently, so the form looks reliable. Walk Away Harry was stepped up to 2m2f at Punchestown later the same month and he won that 18-runner contest from Irish Panther, who is a solid yardstick, with Dr Eggman, a winner next time, back in third. His inexperienced jockey gave him a great ride, waiting patiently for a gap to open up over 1f out but the 5yo galloped on strongly once daylight was found for him. Charles Byrnes said afterwards: "We were a bit concerned the ground today wasn't soft enough for him. The trip helped and he got a brilliant ride." It's likely that a strong gallop and a step up in trip will suit him as he embarks on his hurdling career and it's likely that he will be kept away from good ground too, but there are certainly more races to be won with him. CHARLES BYRNES

WEST BALBOA (IRE) 7 b m

There's a good-quality handicap in West Balboa in the 2023-24 campaign judged on her exploits last season, one that culminated with victory in a competitive 3m event at Aintree on Grand National day. Dan Skelton's mare hasn't had much racing but she's improved with each of her five runs over hurdles, also winning the Lanzarote at Kempton (2m5f, soft) prior to her Aintree success. Following that win at Liverpool, which came after three months off the track, her trainer said: "West Balboa was a fresh horse and that counts for an awful lot. She looked fabulous today and the step up to three miles was always going to be a positive. We always knew we had a very good mare on our hands. The Lanzarote proved that. You have to know when to hold your hand and when to play it and I wasn't ever going to overplay this year. The Mares' Hurdle at Cheltenham was so strong there was no point competing in that to be sixth. Next year she could step up, she could be a player in all those races." Judged on those remarks, she's likely to be going back into non-handicap Graded events at some point and, if her level of progress can be maintained, she's likely to add to her tally. There's also plenty of chase blood in her pedigree if and when her trainer decides to give her a spin over fences. DAN SKELTON

WESTERN DIEGO (IRE) 6 b g

A 3m maiden point winner for Mark Scallan in January 2022, this son of Westerner was sold to the Clipper Logistics Group shortly afterwards before being moved to Willie Mullins. He made his debut for his new trainer about a year later at Naas and he made a very good impression (in a hood) as he put in a professional front-running display to readily see off the consistent Suttons Hill and a well-fancied Gordon Elliott-trained runner, Will Do. That earned him a ticket to Cheltenham and a run in the Champion Bumper and he caught the eye in that race despite only finishing seventh of the twenty-one runners behind A Dream To Share. Ridden by Rachael Blackmore, he took a fearsome hold and led on sufferance about four furlongs from home, having used up plenty of energy to get into that leading position. He was only headed inside the final furlong, however, and then was badly hampered in the run to the finish, which exaggerated the beaten distance, which was ten and three-quarter lengths. It's best to draw a line through his final run of the campaign in the Punchestown Champion Bumper where he led in the early part of the race before being headed after about seven furlongs and then quickly becoming detached, with Derek O'Connor wisely easing him off. He remains a smart prospect for hurdling and he looks sure to be stepped up in trip sooner or later. WILLIE MULLINS

WHITE RHINO (IRE) 7 b g

Oliver Greenall and Josh Guerriero are both former amateur riders who sent out their first runners as joint-licence holders in 2022 and they have quickly made their mark, with Iroko becoming their highest-profile winner so far when taking the Martin Pipe Conditional Jockeys' Handicap Hurdle at the Cheltenham Festival in March. That horse will be an exciting novice chasing prospect for them this season but so will White Rhino, who progressed rapidly over hurdles once sent handicapping earlier this year. He got off the mark at odds of 33/1 at the first time of asking over 2m4f at Southwell in February, beating the odds-on favourite Roger Rarebit in clear-cut fashion, perhaps benefiting from running over a longer trip on better ground, as his three runs in maiden/novice company at the end of 2022 had all come over 2m on ground with 'soft' or 'heavy' in the description. He was turned out under a penalty at Wetherby (2m3f 154y) a week later and he took full advantage of being 10lb well-in by running out a 7l winner. Now rated 93, which is 19lb higher than for his first win, he returned to the scene of his initial victory and completed the hat-trick in good style, with four of the beaten horses franking the form by winning next time (one on the Flat). He ran over the same C&D again one month later off his 10lb higher mark and this time he tasted defeat for the first time in handicaps, although he was far from disgraced in finishing second of thirteen runners to Bertie Blue – he would have finished a good deal closer to that rival had he not made a hash of the last. He could perhaps stay over hurdles in the early part of the new season although he's now rated 35lb higher than when winning his first race in February so a switch to fences will no doubt be on the agenda for him soon. OLIVER GREENALL & JOSH GUERRIERO

WILLMOUNT 5 b g

The winner of a 3m maiden point at Comea in Ireland in February 2022, Willmount was bought for a whopping £340,000 at the Tattersalls Cheltenham sales later the same month on behalf of Olly Harris. A sizeable individual with plenty of scope, we next saw him at Doncaster the following January where he ran out the convincing winner of a bumper over 2m 128y. Thirteen lengths behind him in second was the Nicky Richards-trained Luckie Seven, who would frank the form on his next start by winning a bumper over the same C&D. His then-trainer Neil Mulholland said afterwards: "Willmount will improve from that, he's only a baby. He's a nice horse but he's a long-term prospect and won't go novice hurdling this season." We saw him one more time in a bumper, again at Doncaster in early March, where he gave 22lbs and a four-and-a-half length beating to the Alan King-trained Broomhill Road, with Mulholland saying afterwards: "He's travelled well and can't do any more. We'll have a look at Aintree but we'd want a bit of rain and don't have to run again. If we don't go there we'll put him away." Unfortunately for Mulholland it was the last time Willmount ran for him as he missed Aintree and then in early August Olly Harris decided to move him to Nicky Henderson. His new trainer is also excited by his new recruit: "He will certainly be going straight over hurdles. He's a very nice horse actually and he looked a good horse for Neil last year. He looks very well. He did look a bit special, and interestingly we all knew he looked quite good because I bought his sister at the Derby Sale in Ireland over the summer hoping he might turn out to be a good horse." It is hoped that Henderson can work his magic with this son of Blue Bresil (the same sire as Constitution Hill) and it wouldn't be a huge shock to see this 5yo line up in the Supreme Novices' Hurdle at Cheltenham in March, for which he is currently available at 50/1. NICKY HENDERSON

WINDTOTHELIGHTNING (IRE) 5 b m

Windtothelightning won three of her five starts last season and she's the type to make further progress this time round. The Oliver Greenall & Josh Guerriero-trained mare, who was picked up for £35,000 after finishing second in an Irish point last April, shaped encouragingly when third behind Touchy Feely at Doncaster on her hurdles debut for her new team, form that was franked when the winner went in again at Ludlow the following month. The 5yo showed improved form when winning her next start at Sedgefield two months later and she fairly quickly added victories at Market Rasen (on her handicap debut) and Ayr, also over around 2m4f. The winning run came to a halt back in handicap company on her final start at Cheltenham in April but she nevertheless showed improved form by finishing third to Malaita, keeping on in a manner that suggested she should stay further (backed up by parts of her pedigree). She'll start the season on an official rating of 120, a mark that should give her scope to bag a few more wins in this sphere before a possible tilt over fences. OLIVER GREENALL & JOSH GUERRIERO

YOUNG BUSTER (IRE) 7 b g

Fergal O'Brien has a strong team this season and it will be a big surprise if Young Buster doesn't add to his trainer's tally of winners in the coming months. This soft-ground point winner (from only two outings in that sphere) returned following a lengthy break with a creditable sixth at Aintree last October on his first run for the yard and, although he was not seen for over four months after that (having had wind surgery in the interim), he notched his first rules win at Ffos Las (2m4f, good) over hurdles in March. He matched that effort on his handicap debut when fourth over 3m at Ayr in April but his best effort came when he was switched to fences at Warwick on his final start in May. Although he wasn't fluent at a couple of his obstacles, he created a good impression by beating Quid Pro Quo, who is a reliable yardstick, in convincing fashion over 2m4f. He won't mind a return to further and, although he has yet to prove that he handles extremes of ground, he appeals strongly as the type to do better as a chaser. FERGAL O'BRIEN

YOUR OWN STORY (IRE) 7 b g

Lucinda Russell has quickly made her name with staying chasers, having won the Grand National twice with One For Arthur and Corach Rambler plus the Scottish version with Mighty Thunder in recent years. Although Your Own Story will have to improve a fair bit to become her third Grand National winner, he showed improved form over extreme distances in the first few months of 2023 and he's the type to do better again in the 2023-24 season. This 3m1f hurdle winner has so far only won one of his eight starts over fences (finishing second four times and third once) and that came over 3m6f at Wetherby in March. He matched that run when finishing a close second over 3m4f at Haydock next time and he was far from disgraced in the Scottish National on his final outing at Ayr in April, where he finished sixth of the eighteen runners behind Kitty's Light. He seems to go on any ground so the slog that is usually the Welsh National could be under consideration as a mid-season target. Failing that, the Eider Chase at Newcastle could be an option, although he'll have to improve a fair bit if he's to make the cut for the Grand National itself. Whatever the plan is, though, he's likely to give a good account of himself when things turn into a proper test of stamina. LUCINDA RUSSELL

RACING POST

The highly popular Racing Post calendars feature stunning racing photos taken by the Racing Post's award-winning photographers.

Each calendar features one month to view and includes the most up-to-date race meeting information in the UK and Ireland at the time of publication, and highlights the key races each month.

Racing Post's *Unforgettable Moments Wall Calendar 2024* features stunning and evocative racing photos from the Racing Post archives and will stir up memories from racing's history for all fans of the sport.

EW SHOP WEBSITE LIVE NOW!

ww.racingpost.com/shop

INDEX

100 WINNERS
HORSES TO FOLLOW FLAT
2024

Companion volume to **100 Winners: Jumpers to Follow**, this book discusses the past performances and future prospects of 100 horses, selected by Raceform's expert race-readers, that are likely to perform well on the Flat in 2024.

To order post the coupon to the address below or order online from **www.racingpost.com/shop**

Tel 01933 304848

ORDER FORM

Please send me a copy of **100 WINNERS: HORSES TO FOLLOW FLAT 2024** as soon as it is published. I enclose a cheque made payable to Pitch Publishing Ltd for **£7.99** (inc p&p)

Name (block capitals) ....

Address ....

....

Postcode ....

SEND TO: PITCH PUBLISHING,

SANDERS ROAD, WELLINGBOROUGH, NORTHANTS NN8 4BX [100F24]